MONROVIA
MON AMOUR

A VISIT TO LIBERIA

MONROVIA MON AMOUR

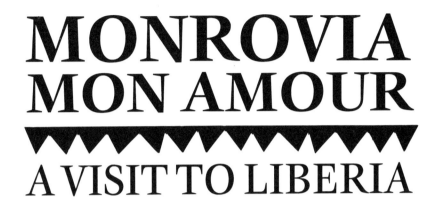

A VISIT TO LIBERIA

ANTHONY DANIELS

JOHN MURRAY

© Anthony Daniels 1992

First published in 1992
by John Murray (Publishers) Ltd
50 Albemarle Street, London W1X 4BD

The moral right of the author has been asserted

A catalogue record for this book is available from the British Library

ISBN 0–7195–5025–4

Typeset in 11½/14pt Times Roman by
Wearset, Boldon, Tyne & Wear
Printed and bound in Great Britain by Bookcraft Ltd.

CONTENTS

ILLUSTRATIONS

(between pages 96 and 97)

All photographs are by the author.

ACKNOWLEDGEMENTS

I should like to thank the following people for their help in the preparation of this book: Miss Elizabeth Blunt and Mr Alex Vincenti of the BBC World Service, London; Mr Scott Stearns of the BBC in Monrovia; Mr James Dio Bollie of Monrovia; Mr Alistair Kerr of the British Embassy, Abidjan; Captain Monty Jones of Lomé; Mr Eugene Cooper of Monrovia; Mr Will Davis, formerly of Monrovia, now of Washington DC; and Mr David Weir of Yesterday's Books, Bournemouth.

Any errors in this book are, of course, my own.

I should also like to thank my editor, Mr Roger Hudson, and my friends Mr Ingo and Dr Helen Evers for their hospitality in Shropshire during the writing of *Monrovia Mon Amour*. They listened patiently to more about Liberia than they ever thought to hear.

1

A TUG TO MONROVIA

On the morning of my arrival in the Ivory Coast I learned that the *Steel Trader* was due to sail from Abidjan for Monrovia and I went straight down to the 'Port Autonome'. A man in khaki uniform, reclining on a bench like Madame Récamier, barred my way. I was not allowed to enter the port.

'Where are you going?' he asked.

'The *Steel Trader*,' I replied.

'Why?'

'I am a doctor,' I said, leaving open the possibility that a terrible epidemic had broken out on board.

'Do you have medicine with you?' asked the official.

'Of course,' I said.

'I am always tired, doctor,' said the guardian of port security.

'Why?' I asked.

Laboriously, he levered himself up on to his elbow.

'Too much work,' he said.

I searched in my box of time-expired medicaments for something suitable, and alighted on erythromicin, vivid pink antibiotic pills that looked as though they would glow in the dark.

'These', I said, 'are very good for tiredness.'

'How many do I take?' he asked.

'One a day, until you are no longer tired.'

'Merci. Bon voyage, docteur,' said the official, collapsing back on to his bench.

That was the end of immigration and customs formalities in Abidjan.

The *Steel Trader* was a twenty-year-old tug under the command of Captain Monty Jones, a Welshman who had lived more than half his life up and down the coast of West Africa. A man of parts, he was now Her Majesty's Honorary Consul at Lomé in Togo. A contract had been put out on him in Lomé by an Algerian businessman there, whose British wife he had recently rescued from the jealous captivity in which the Algerian held her. At the height of the Liberian civil war, when Monrovia was virtually cut off from the rest of the world, Monty's had been the only ship willing to brave Monrovia harbour. Freight rates then were so high that Monty had made a small fortune, but at the same time he had probably saved thousands of people from starvation. The *Steel Trader* towed a large barge which Monty had bought at a knock-down price in Nigeria, where it had spent eight years aground on the banks of the River Niger. The Nigerians had bought several such barges from West Germany, not for use (they had never been used), but for the kick-backs consequent upon the signing of the contract. Now Monty was taking food and medicine to Liberia, and picking up diplomatic effects from closing embassies, including the British Ambassador's Range Rover, which he had bought for next to nothing.

There were two other white men on board. The first was Rambo, a bearded Vietnam veteran and former US marine who longed for action and spent most of his free time in his cabin lovingly polishing his formidable arsenal of weaponry.

He had enjoyed the Liberian civil war, because in those days pirates would attack the ship off the Liberian coast and he could fire at them with an automatic (he was a crack shot). He would also fight off the starving thieves who swarmed on board to steal the food as it arrived in the harbour, running up and down the barge wielding a club and yelling like a banshee. Monty, no pacifist, had to tell him to go easy. When the *Steel Trader* arrived in Monrovia at the height of the civil war, with artillery shells exploding overhead, the water of the harbour bobbed with bodies, hundreds of them, and Rambo gave them names. 'Look,' he would say, 'there's Albert again' – Albert being headless. Rambo had a large collection of extra-bloody war videos in his cabin, and most of what little conversation he made related to war. He was disappointed that conditions had normalized somewhat in Monrovia, and there was nothing for him to do in the way of protection work. Monty, to keep him happy, would ask him to stand guard outside the bar in which he drank and Rambo, doggedly loyal, would do so, ready to pounce on anyone who lifted a finger against his master. When a Russian trawler came in sight, Monty teased him by telling him to keep a close eye on it, since Russian trawlers were never what they seemed; and Rambo, unaware of the end of the Cold War, trained his binoculars suspiciously on the ship, which he was certain was a spy vessel. When the Monrovia harbour pilot came out to meet us on his motor launch, Rambo said, 'An AK–47 would do a beautiful job on that boat,' and he meant it.

The second white man was Serge, a Frenchman of solid proportions. Serge was now penniless and on the run from a Togolese gaol, travelling without papers, except for some issued by a complaisant humanitarian aid organization. A less likely looking humanitarian it would be difficult to imagine; his corpulence was bear-like, solid and muscular, and he always had a cigarette attached by dried saliva to his lower lip, a method of smoking which somehow invariably conveys an air of sophisticated knowingness. Sometimes he would appear on the bridge of the *Steel Trader* in a Red Cross T-shirt, which was irresistibly comic. Serge had once been Valéry Giscard d'Estaing's personal bodyguard, and had travelled with him throughout Africa. He had fought in Zaire, where he saw cannibalism at first hand, and had been present at the Emperor Bokassa's coronation. ('It was we, the French who paid for it, who were mad, not Bokassa,' said Serge.) Serge had made a lot of money in Togo, but the minister with whom he was associated fell from grace with the president, which meant that Serge lost everything and was hounded as a criminal. Monty muttered something about Serge and an arms deal; and Serge said that if he wrote a book of all that he knew (including the very numbers of the bank accounts into which payments had been made), not only the president of Togo, but the president of France himself, would fall the next day. But it was too dangerous to write such a book, for politics – said Serge – was a dirty business, and the only difference between Europe and Africa was that in the former, things – by which he meant murder – were arranged more discreetly.

Serge was born in the French Congo, before air conditioning. Although it was hard to visualize Serge as a child, let alone as a baby, he told me that his mother used to wrap him in a wet sheet at night to keep him cool and to protect him from the mosquitoes. Serge was scathing about life in present-day France, which he found insufferably well-ordered and smug. He had gone 'home' on holiday two years before, intending to stay three months, but he lasted only a week. 'What is life in France?' he asked. 'You work

14

all week for eleven months just for one month's holiday. On Saturday you rush to the supermarket. On Sunday you have lunch with your mother-in-law. I have relatives in France who, when their company moved thirty kilometres away, preferred to be unemployed than move themselves.' Serge, whose life was movement, could think of nothing more contemptible. He was going to Liberia to start all over again; though he spoke no English, he was thinking of becoming bodyguard to Prince Johnson (one of the leaders there during the civil war). 'It isn't difficult to make money,' he said. 'The difficulty is to keep it.'

Monty told me a story about Serge, the moral of which is still not quite clear to me. A French television crew of left-liberal leanings arrived in Togo determined to make a film about the ugly side of the white man in Africa. They asked Serge whether, for 100,000 CFA francs (£200), he would approach a black man in the street, insult him and smack him on the face in front of their cameras. Serge agreed; he walked up to a passer-by and aimed a blow at him. He fell to the ground, and Serge demanded his 100,000 francs. The crew gave him the money, and as the unfortunate man stood up, Serge gave him 5000 francs.

'Merci, patron,' said the man, delighted at his good luck.

Serge was a survivor. There was something magnificent about the way he coped with his reversal of fortune, about his lack of bitterness over his plunge from a position of wealth and influence to his present state of penury and outlawry. It was life and adventure that Serge loved, not power and money, and he lived by a creed that most men can only theorize or dream about. He was a true romantic.

Monty, too, was admirable. He was a swashbuckler who risked much and gained much: his decisions were his own, and he would never have blamed others for his mistakes. He

15

gloried in his new-found wealth, and he loved to go home to his village in Wales to display it. Like all traders in West Africa, he had known downs as well as ups; he had, for example, been imprisoned in Guinea, no trivial experience. (Serge and he once had a discussion about which was the worst place in the world, Chad, Mauretania or Guinea.) Like Serge, he was a free man.

Ashamed of myself in such company, I was seasick on the first day out of Abidjan, despite the calmness of the sea. I recovered, however, and was then able to enjoy the beauty of the blue water, of the flying fish that broke the surface and glided hundreds of yards at high speed, and of the dolphins that played around the stem of the boat, almost as if they craved human company. I began even to enjoy the excellent food on board. Monty was a swashbuckler, but he kept – as he said – 'a proper ship'.

It took us eighty-four hours to reach Monrovia. The sea, as I constantly reminded myself, is a big place. On the way we passed Buchanan, the second port of Liberia, now in the hands of rebels led by Charles Taylor. Ships steamed in and out of the port, despite its rebel status, taking away the iron ore, timber and diamonds that almost certainly paid for the Libyan arms, smuggled through Burkina Faso, which sustained Taylor's drive for power.

We arrived in Monrovia in darkness. The city had no electricity, except for the former diplomatic enclave at Mamba Point. All embassies, except the American, had closed down (the British, the first to recognize Liberian independence in 1847, had departed the week before, never – for reasons of economy – to return). The diplomatic quarter and its generators had been taken over by the aid organizations that arrive in the wake of any disaster. High on the hill around which Mamba Point was built was the

16

Ducor Palace Hotel, a fine example of the depressingly ugly architecture of the 1960s, now the seat of the Interim Government of National Unity, whose writ ran only in the city of Monrovia itself, and then only by the grace of the West African peace keeping troops (known as ECOMOG) who had been sent by Nigeria, Ghana, Gambia, Sierra Leone and Guinea to prevent the Liberian conflict from spreading to the whole of West Africa. As someone remarked to me, things have to be desperate if you are pleased to see Nigerians with guns.

ECOMOG had succeeded in imposing some kind of order on the capital, much to the disappointment of Rambo. And Monty was thinking of pulling out of the Monrovia run because his arch-rival along the West African coast, a larger cargo vessel, had suddenly lowered its freight rate to a figure which made it no longer profitable for Monty. This ship, the *Westseas*, was berthed at the quayside when we arrived, and as the darkness lifted we could see how it had been able to lower the freight rate so precipitously. The deck of the *Westseas* was laden with heavy construction equipment, looted during the civil war, which the owners of the ship proposed to export from Liberia to the Ivory Coast at the very time the equipment was most needed in Liberia. It was completely illegal, of course, but the potential profits were enormous. Unfortunately for the owners of the ship (and for us), ECOMOG had got wind of the scheme; and they had therefore refused the *Westseas* permission to sail until some of the profits were handed over to them. The negotiations over the amount to be paid took a whole day, and as we were to berth at the same quay as the *Westseas*, we had to ride at anchor for that time.

Eventually, however, it sailed away, and the harbour pilot joined us to guide us in. There were bullet holes in the

17

window of his boat's bridge. Rambo proposed to add considerably to them, on the grounds that the pilot, like everyone else, would soon extract dash (in his case, a sack of flour). As for the harbour, it was dotted with sunken boats. A tug stood high and dry on a small beach. Someone once asked why Liberian soldiers shot so much into the sea. The answer came back at once: 'It's the only thing they can hit.'

As we tied up by the quayside officials came aboard, all eager for their bribes. There was a problem with my passport – I had no entry visa. It is true there was still a Liberian Embassy in London (whose telephones, however, could only receive calls and not make them, since the bill had not been paid for a year or two), and that the Embassy was more than willing to issue me with a visa within twenty-four hours, but the question arose as to whether anyone in Liberia would recognize its validity, since the staff of the Embassy were still appointees of Samuel Doe, who had been killed seven months before. As Elizabeth Blunt of the BBC told me, any Liberian Embassy would stamp my passport if I paid (the sale of visas being their only source of income), but the effect such a stamp would have in Liberia was uncertain. The Liberian Embassy also politely requested documentary evidence that I was not a criminal, was of good character, and suffered from no infections or mental diseases. This seemed to me a trifle fastidious for a country in which over half the population had been displaced by civil war and untold thousands had died. I approached my hospital for a certificate of good character, but the bureaucrat there qualified his testimonial by the words 'as far as is known'. I decided to write my own glowing reference, but in the end there was no time to use it. In any case, the diplomats at the Embassy found the whole idea of going voluntarily to Liberia faintly preposterous.

'You do know,' they said, 'that there's been a spot of trouble out there?'

Evidently, they had been a long time in England.

I was left, therefore, to spend several hours on the quayside, waiting for the wheels of the rump of Liberian bureaucracy to grind. Opposite was the green port office building to which Samuel Doe, as the overthrown President of Liberia, had driven for an agreed meeting with Prince Johnson, only to be captured and seventy of his men killed. The nearby warehouses and sheds looked battered and damaged, but I was informed by those who knew Monrovia well that they had been well on the way to their present state of decay even before the civil war broke out. The only real war damage was the occasional hole in their fabric caused by a stray missile.

There was not the chaos and the frantic rush for food that had occurred in the last months of 1990 and the first months of 1991. In those days, rice had sold for up to $1000 a hundred-pound bag, and there was a story of a looted Mercedes being exchanged for two such bags. A thief had stuffed his pockets with so much stolen rice from the *Steel Trader* that, when he jumped into the water to escape with his booty, he sank and drowned. The people then had looked starved and desperate; but now, as the *Steel Trader* was unloaded under the eyes of ECOMOG soldiers, there were no untoward events. Only a small group of mal-nourished children hovered round the quay, waiting for an opportunity to scoop up the flour that was inevitably spilled on to the ground, and eating it straight from their hands. But the most noticeable people on the quay were the aid workers, who arrived in brand-new vehicles which glittered like diamonds among dross. I could not but recall Malabo, the capital of Equatorial Guinea, where in the wake of

19

another man-made disaster I had amused myself for a time by counting the number of different aid agencies whose vehicles I could spot. I gave up after twenty. There were now twenty-seven such agencies in Monrovia, I was told, but (my cynicism notwithstanding) there was no doubt they had averted a disaster of even greater proportions in the city, especially those, such as Médecins Sans Frontières, which had operated at great risk throughout the worst times.

Eventually, and mysteriously, my passport reappeared. I bid farewell to the captain, who was not at all downcast by the improvement of conditions in Monrovia. The whole coast was seething with discontent; both Sierra Leone and Guinea were ready to explode at any moment, whereupon the *Steel Trader* would regain its monopoly position. And the amelioration in Liberia might well prove temporary, a mere lull before the resumption of the storm; altogether, Monty was confident there would be work for him to do in the not too distant future.

And now I was on my own – or nearly so, since two of the ship's crew carried my baggage to the port gate, automatically as it were, on the assumption that white men did not carry things. *En route* to the gate, I changed money. There were no banks open in Monrovia, and the rate of exchange at the port was more favourable than with the Lebanese businessmen of the city. Until the presidency of Samuel Doe, Liberia had issued no currency of its own, except for coins, US dollars being legal tender. Doe had come to power promising wage increases for the lowly paid in government, a promise he kept; but since there was insufficient revenue to meet this expenditure (especially after Doe had finished with it), he soon resorted to printing dollars of his own, which were popularly known as 'Doebucks'. Not surprisingly, these did not long keep their parity with the US currency, and now the rate was 6.5 to 1. The banknotes carried a portrait of J. J. Roberts, the first President of Liberia – who, as one American remarked to me, was certainly the whitest-looking black man in history, if the portrait on the banknotes was to be believed.

Outside the port was a bustling street market scene: the city was coming to life again, despite the absence of electricity, telephones, running water, postal services, public transport or banks. At this stage, of course, I did not realize that everything for sale by the side of the road – everything – had been looted. People later told me that they often found their own property in the street, but they appeared to have overcome their anger; so universal had been the looting, and so necessary to survival, that it seemed to be the result of a force of nature rather than of human agency.

The walls of the buildings along the road to the city were pock-marked, as though by epidemic disease – wallpox. The damage had been done, of course, by bullets. Almost every window had been smashed, leaving jagged patterns like the designs of a *passé* abstract artist, and the shutters of the shops and showrooms had long been drawn down. The question was, would they ever go up again? The produce by the side of the road was all imported and now Monrovia, which was completely cut off from the rest of the country, had nothing to sell the rest of the world to pay for further imports. It was living off its dwindling capital, and on foreign aid.

Monrovia is built at the outlet of the Mesurado River, and its geography is complex. The rusting shacks by the riverside had been less affected by the war than the more formal parts of the city: they looked much as I assumed they had always done, dirty, crowded, blackened by age and smoke, sinks of iniquity and disease, no doubt, but nevertheless not without

21

a certain charm, at least from a distance.

I put up at the Hotel El Meson, owned and run by Lebanese, on Carey Street. (It was named after the Revd Lott Carey, one of the first Governors of Liberia. I explained to several Liberians that, in England, to say that someone was in Carey Street was to say he was bankrupt, because the bankruptcy court had once sat there. Somehow, one's thoughts turned easily to bankruptcy in Liberia.) The El Meson had been recommended to me first because it was open, whereas practically all other hotels in Monrovia had been destroyed, and second because it was splendidly louche. I was told that in the morning there were scenes of Hogarthian decadence in the half-dark bar, with ladies of the evening in crimson satin dresses draped around Lebanese businessmen drinking pink champagne for breakfast. Alas, I saw no crimson dresses, or pink champagne for that matter, though there were quite a number of prostitutes. On the whole, the war seemed to have made El Meson respectable, the meeting place of well-paid workers with nowhere else to go.

The humid heat of Monrovia had made me thirsty, to put it mildly, and I had a drink at the bar. I noticed at once that it was well-stocked with those emergency goods that are imported after any catastrophe involving widespread death and destruction: Johnny Walker Black Label, Marlboro cigarettes, Saint Emilion. I suppose that, in the circumstances, it was outrageous, but I realized with relief that I was not going to suffer too much during my stay in Monrovia: I could safely throw away the packet of dried prunes which had constituted my sole effort to equip myself for hardship. In any case, dried prunes invariably bring out streams of tiny ants in tropical hotel bedrooms, which can penetrate any package known to man, and render prunes

22

even less appetising than they already are. The questions I have never been able to answer are, what are these ants doing, and where are they, before the prunes arrive?

I went out on to the balcony of El Meson to survey the scene. Across Carey Street was the City Hotel, burnt out. Apparently, the soldiers set fire to it while there were still guests in it. Stouffer's Bar (where, somewhat incongruously, the Monrovia Chess Club had its headquarters) was likewise closed. To the left were the ruins of the Mayfair Amusement Club (Poker Machine & Slot Machine), the Star Grill and Restaurant and Sweet Heart Pastries. All these were now mere façades: the buildings behind had been totally destroyed and reduced to rubble, overlaid with piles of rubbish.

I took my first walk in the city. There is one thing to be said in favour of a sacked city: afterwards, it is very quiet. There was little traffic in central Monrovia; many of the owners of cars had departed, and the cars themselves were destroyed, left by the side of the road in various states of desolation. There were cars without windows, cars without wheels, cars without bodies, cars on blocks, cars upside down, cars rusted away. In an avant-garde art gallery they might have excited the praises of the critics for 'their imaginative variation on a single theme, itself deeply symbolic of our disturbed century, so technically proficient, so humanly primitive'.

I heard an unexpected sound – laughter – emerging from the ruins as the light began to fade. People were rebuilding their lives, as though after a storm. Is mankind like grass, that grows up again immediately upon being mown down? Because of the lack of traffic, the streets were safe for the children playing football. People sat in doorways, chatting quietly as if nothing had happened. And ruins have their attractions, especially for children. As darkness fell, the only sound in the unlit streets was a languorous murmur of conversation. To be in a city and yet be in utter darkness – that was something new, and in an odd way refreshing, for I am sure the lights of Monrovia had been garish and commonplace.

On Broad Street, the wide main thoroughfare of the city that leads towards the Ducor Palace, I passed the Catholic Cathedral, one of the few buildings untouched by the fighting. I listened outside to a service that was being conducted by an Irish priest; he talked of sin and redemption. On the outdoor noticeboard of the Cathedral was a faded poster from a long-forgotten era of almost absurd moral sensibility. 'Abortion', it said, 'is murder.'

2

A BRIEF HISTORY OF LIBERIA

A little knowledge, especially of history, is a dangerous thing, for it easily leads to false and desperate political conclusions. Nevertheless, what one sees around one is often incomprehensible unless at least something is known of how it came to be; and nowhere is this more so than in Liberia, where the destruction of Monrovia might otherwise appear utterly senseless. But it is *not* senseless – unless greed and the instinct for survival be senseless.

Liberia was founded in the first quarter of the nineteenth century as a colony for freed slaves from the United States. The whites who favoured the establishment of such a colony in Africa were by no means the disinterested friends of the black man they are sometimes portrayed as having been: more than anything, they feared the disturbing example that free men of colour would be to those who remained slaves (the revolt of Spartacus, and the then recent revolution in Haiti, in the course of which the whites were massacred, were never far from the slave-owners' minds). Those who foresaw the inevitable end of slavery feared for the subsequent purity of the white race in the United States, upon which the prosperity and greatness of the country were thought to depend. Some dreamed of returning all the black men in North America to Africa, but in the event no more than a few thousand ever re-emigrated to the continent of their forefathers. A few thousand more colonists were put ashore by the United States Navy, which intercepted slave-trading ships along the coasts of Africa. This explains why the Americo-Liberians are sometimes known in Liberia as 'the Congo people', or 'Congos', but strictly speaking this is an error: the intercepted slaves were different from true Americo-Liberians, and the social distinction between them (so I was told) has remained to this day.

In 1847 the colony, until then a dependency of the American Colonization Society, declared its independence. The Liberian Declaration of Independence is generally regarded as a verbose and slightly ridiculous document, a degenerate plagiarism of the American equivalent of seventy years earlier; but its explanation of why the Liberian experiment was undertaken by the freed slaves is surely heartfelt:

We . . . were originally inhabitants of the United States of North America.

In some parts of that country we were debarred by law from all rights and privileges of man – in other parts, public sentiment, more powerful than law, frowned us down.

We were everywhere shut out from all civil office.

We were excluded from all participation in the Government.

We were taxed without our consent.

We were compelled to contribute to the resources of a country which gave us no protection.

We were made a separate and distinct class, and against us every avenue of improvement was effectually closed.

Strangers from other lands, of a colour different from

ours, were preferred before us.

We uttered our complaints, but they were unattended to, or only met by alleging the peculiar institutions of the country.

All hope of a favourable change in our country was thus wholly extinguished in our bosoms, and we looked with anxiety for some asylum from this deep degradation.

The Americo-Liberians at this time numbered not more than six thousand. But Liberia was no *tabula rasa*: the land was already inhabited by a score of tribes, and the native population vastly outnumbered the colonists. This fact at once introduced ambiguity into the noble principles the latter espoused, in the same way as the existence of slavery had introduced it into the American Declaration of Independence. Were the aboriginal inhabitants of Liberia citizens or not? Despite this difficult question, the colonists were confident of success, and the first Liberian constitution, written by a Harvard professor called Greenleaf, contained a clause concerning the encouragement of agriculture and husbandry among the natives.

The first President of Liberia, J. J. Roberts, himself an octoroon (which explains his caucasian appearance on the five-Doebuck banknote), had no doubts about the benefits to the natives of the introduction to them of Christianity and European civilization, and no doubts either about the cultural superiority of the settlers to the natives. He did not mince his words; in his inaugural address as President, he said:

And, as the political happiness or wretchedness of ourselves and our children, and of generations yet unborn, is in our hands, nay more, the redemption of Africa from the deep degradation, superstition, and idolatry in which she has so long been involved, it becomes us to lay our shoulders to the wheel, and manfully resist every obstacle which may oppose our progress in the great work that lies before us. The Gospel, fellow citizens, is yet to be preached to vast numbers inhabiting this dark continent, and I have the highest reason to believe, that it was one of the great objects of the Almighty in establishing these colonies, that they might be the means of introducing civilization and religion among the barbarous nations of this country . . .

These sentiments would not meet with much approval nowadays, perhaps; but they are not intrinsically more absurd, and are probably more sincerely felt, than many of the later protestations of negritude, invariably expressed in a European language and addressed, as often as not, to a European audience. At the heart of the Liberian problem is a conflict of identity, between European thought and African feeling: a conflict which the Americo-Liberians were unable to resolve. About this failure they need feel no shame, since no one else on the continent has succeeded any better than they.

The Americo-Liberians dominated Liberia politically and economically for 133 years, the latter 104 of them through the good offices of the True Whig Party. The last two presidents under the old dispensation, William Vacanarat Shadrach Tubman and William Richard Tolbert, Junior, sometime pastor of the Bensonville Zion Praise Baptist Church and President of the World Baptist Alliance, ruled for thirty-six years between them. They brought economic development and social change to Liberia: one has only to read accounts of the country written shortly before their accession to power to realize the extent of the transformation they wrought, or at least presided over.

Times of change, even for the better, are dangerous times, however; for the changes are never sufficient for the dreamers and thinkers. So it was in Liberia, where the corruption and nepotism of the *ancien régime* were plain to see, but where progress was taken for granted the moment it was made. There was oppression too, of a comparatively mild nature, and there were absurd elections, fawning courtiers and silly slogans (Tolbert said he was building 'A Wholesome Functioning Society'); no one valued the peace that reigned for many years or stopped to ask himself whether an uncorrupt and un-nepotistic Liberia was a realistic possibility. In 1979, riots convulsed Monrovia when Tolbert (whose family firm was said to be the biggest commercial importer of rice in the country) proposed an increase in the price of rice. In the aftermath of the riots, Tolbert reduced the price to below the original figure, but the regime was badly shaken. A year later almost to the day, a coup led by the then Master Sergeant Samuel Kanyon Doe destroyed the immemorial dominance of the Americo-Liberians; Tolbert was killed and thirteen of his ministers were shot soon afterwards on the beach. Doe and his sixteen co-conspirators, all non-commissioned officers, formed what they called 'The People's Redemption Council'.

A Romanian proverb says that a change of rulers is the joy of fools; and everyone in Liberia (except the Americo-Liberians) rejoiced. Doe was immensely popular at first: he promised the lowly-paid soldiers and government workers increases in their wages, and much else beside. The intellectuals joined his government and, considering him but a simple, semi-literate sort of fellow, thought they would manipulate him easily. But Doe soon began to grow fat, a bad sign in a West African ruler, and with his increasing girth came increasing suspiciousness. He imagined plots all around him, and used them as pretexts for ridding himself of his erstwhile companions and associates. Soon, most of the intellectuals were in exile; Doe replaced them with members of his own Krahn tribe. Eventually, there was a real plot against him, led by the exiled General (formerly Sergeant) Thomas Quiwonkpa, one of the original members of The People's Redemption Council. (Of the seventeen members of the Council, at least thirteen were dead only ten years later – and they were all young men.) Quiwonkpa invaded Liberia from Sierra Leone with a group of would-be revolutionaries. He was caught, chopped into pieces and – according to one eyewitness – eaten on the streets of Monrovia.

Quiwonkpa came from Nimba County, to the north-east of Monrovia, inhabited by the Gio and Mano tribes, whom Doe decided to teach a lesson. His army, by now overwhelmingly of the Krahn tribe, rampaged through Nimba County, killing thousands of innocent people. Thus was an irreconcilable hatred sealed between the Krahn and the Gio and Mano, upon which the leader of the present rebellion, Charles Taylor, seized to further his personal ambitions.

Charles Taylor is an Americo-Liberian with a degree in economics from the United States. In spite of his ethnic origins, he was given an important appointment in The People's Redemption Council government: he was placed in charge of all government purchasing, a position from which he was soon able to embezzle millions. Eventually, his defalcations became so gross that he was forced to flee Liberia; he went to the United States, where he was imprisoned for a time and then jumped bail (he remains on the wanted list there). West Africa, however, still offered wide scope for a man of his talents, and it is rumoured that he was instrumental in the overthrow and murder of Thomas Sankara, the President of Burkina Faso, which lies to the north of Liberia's eastern neighbour, The Ivory Coast. At any rate, it is certain that the beneficiary of Sankara's death, his former friend and now President of Burkina Faso, Blaise Campaore, is a friend of Taylor's. Campaore has allowed Taylor to use Burkina as a base for his operations.

The arms for Taylor's insurrectionary organization, the National Patriotic Front of Liberia, came (and come) from Libya, whose leader, Colonel Gadaffi, is ever-willing to fish in troubled waters, especially if it will cause annoyance or embarrassment to the Americans. Furthermore, Doe's élite forces were trained by the Israelis, with whom Doe maintained good relations, thus giving Gadaffi a further reason for supporting his enemies.

Doe, meanwhile, had made another powerful enemy, President Felix Houphuet-Boigny of The Ivory Coast. Houphuet-Boigny's stepdaughter had married Tolbert's son, whom Doe killed in his coup. Houphuet-Boigny was not pleased to lose his son-in-law in this fashion, and he therefore allowed Taylor to use The Ivory Coast to launch his attacks. To compound matters, Houphuet-Boigny's stepdaughter soon remarried . . . President Campaore of Burkina Faso.

Thus personal ambition, thirst for revenge and tribal hatreds were inextricably intertwined in the Liberian civil war. Taylor recruited to his cause ten- and twelve-year-old children, many of whom had seen their own parents killed by Doe's troops. He also recruited Prince Johnson, a former preacher in the army, who had undergone military training both in Libya and at Fort Bragg, North Carolina.

Taylor was at first regarded as a liberator, so hated was Doe. The Armed Forces of Liberia, the official Liberian army which Doe had made his own, offered little resistance until the rebel forces reached Monrovia where, once cornered, they stood and fought. At this point Johnson broke with Taylor and became his mortal enemy. He formed his own Independent National Patriotic Front of Liberia.

Johnson captured Doe by subterfuge and killed him. Most Liberians hoped that Doe's death would signal the end of the war, but the question arose as to who was to succeed him as head of state. Taylor, whose ambitions had always been presidential, would accept nothing less than the Interim Presidency, until elections could be held; but Liberians, after Doe, were suspicious of liberators and coup-makers who wished to be president until elections could be held. Doe had turned himself into a civilian in 1985, and had had himself made President in elections as blatantly fraudulent as any organized by the True Whig Party.

Taylor was unable to dislodge the Armed Forces of Liberia from the centre of Monrovia. His men (and boys), dressed in bizarre costumes which momentarily captured the imagination of the world, behaved with exemplary brutality, killing not only any Krahn they could find, but any employees, however humble, of the Doe government. It did not take long for the people of the city to realize that Taylor was no improvement on Doe. Meanwhile, the Armed Forces of Liberia, having lost their leader and fearing annihilation, acted upon the slogan, 'No Doe, No Monrovia'. For once, a slogan in Africa meant something: there was an orgy of destruction.

Some of the nearby West African states grew alarmed at the spreading anarchy, which could so easily have spilled over the borders of Liberia and destroyed the feeble polities of countries such as Guinea and Sierra Leone. Nigeria, anxious to play the part of great power in the region, took the lead; a cease-fire was arranged, the army was confined to barracks in Monrovia, Prince Johnson's men were confined to a camp in a suburb of Monrovia called Caldwell, and Taylor's forces retired to a line just beyond Monrovia. An Interim Government of National Unity, whose legitimacy Taylor did not recognize, whose writ did not run beyond the confines of the capital, and which governed its tiny enclave entirely by the grace and favour of the West African peace keeping force (ECOMOG), was organized, headed by an academic political scientist, Dr Amos Sawyer. The fighting and the killing, at least for the time being, ceased.

I arrived in Monrovia during the fragile interregnum: no war, but no peace. Nothing had been resolved; Charles Taylor was still holding out for supreme power, which he felt was his due because of his part in the removal of Doe. He was not a freedom fighter, however, as he liked to portray himself: he was, rather, a Swiss bank account fighter.

3

UNIVERSITY LIFE

Ruins, as the Romantics knew very well, exert an attraction
all their own, for they are a bitter-sweet reminder of the
transience of human existence and of the irrevocable passage of time; and on the morning after my arrival I went, not
without a certain pleasurable anticipation, to explore the
ruins of Monrovia. I was fortunate to find a Liberian driver
who seemed to know by instinct what would interest me
and, though it was an interest he could scarcely share, being
so remote from his own daily concerns, he remained patient
and loyal throughout my archaeological researches.

I have tramped over the remains of many an ancient
civilization, and have inspected the damage done to several
modern cities by earthquake and flood, but nowhere I have
been has remotely resembled Monrovia. It must once have
been a pleasant place, refreshingly free of that architectural
gigantism that Africans (and not only Africans) so frequent-
ly mistake for progress and modernity. The predominant
style of building in the better part of Monrovia owed its
inspiration to the southern United States of the last century;
houses were built of red brick, with tall arches at the front to
provide broad verandahs on both ground and upper floors.
It was not great architecture, but it was adapted to the
climate, it was pleasing to the eye and it was on a human

scale. It was difficult to associate it with savagery.

Many of these houses were ruins, of course, mere shells. They looked fragile, as if a good kick would bring them crashing down. Their tin roofs were torn off, their windows blown out. Their doors, lintels, beams and window frames had been extracted for use as firewood. The floors were deeply covered with rubble; there was not a stick of furniture left in the rooms, not an ornament to show that people, with their own peculiar tastes, memories and preoccupations, had once lived in them. The land around them, once garden, had returned to wilderness, a petty jungle of coarse grass and stunted shrubs. Sometimes a rusted hulk of a car lay in the grass: I was reminded of pictures of old Japanese fighters from the Second World War slowly decomposing in the forests of New Guinea. I stopped to photograph one of the houses, and some children ran out: they wanted their photograph taken. Whole families were camping out in the ruins, like barbarians who had just conquered and sacked a city of a higher civilization whose citizens had fled or been killed.

Up on the brow of Mamba Point was the Ducor Palace Hotel, where the Interim Government of National Unity had its seat. A little way below it was the once grand, or grandiose, Masonic building, with a portico of Corinthian and Ionic columns. It had been a symbol of the dominance of the America-Liberians, so that on Doe's accession to power it had been sacked, looted and gutted. It had once been sparkling white, but in the decade of Doe's rule it had turned dirty grey (in the second half of his term, Doe himself became a Freemason). On the roof was a large wire globe, no doubt a Masonic symbol of deep significance. Outside, a forlorn statue of one of the Grand Masters of Liberian Masonry stood with one arm outstretched towards the ruined building, the pedestal recording the names of previous Grand Masters. The building had no windows now, no electricity, and no water supply; it was occupied by a detachment of the ECOMOG peace keeping force.

We sought out the officer commanding the detachment, to ask permission to go round the building. We were met by a soldier of inferior rank, who led us up a grand sweeping stone staircase, curiously at odds with the bareness of the floors, and of the walls, from which even the light switches had been removed, leaving short lengths of wire protruding. The soldier took us to a room across whose doorway, in the absence of a door, a curtain had been crudely strung. Behind the curtain I caught a glimpse of two young ladies, dressed in cheap finery. The captain emerged, none too pleased to see us, and very suspicious. He was dressed in a T-shirt and shorts, and looked as if the night before had been an unrestful one.

I explained that I wanted to see round the building, a desire he found incomprehensible and therefore highly suspect. The building was a ruin, nothing more, providing temporary shelter for his men; what reason could anyone have for wishing to tour it? I explained that it was historic, that several presidents of Liberia had been Grand Masters of the Masonic order, and so forth, but still he shook his head in incomprehension. These white men were strange. However, he eventually agreed to my request, on condition that I asked no questions of his soldiers, should I meet any. The few whom I later glimpsed were in any case too busy entertaining young ladies to answer any questions; the ladies, I assumed, were relieving them of their pay. (Only later did I learn that many of the soldiers had not been paid for three months.)

The captain was right, however: there was little to see in

the Masonic building. It had been stripped so bare that there was nothing left upon which the imagination could work. Only in the deserted basement did I find some memento of former times. There, small plaques placed upon the walls had not been destroyed; reading them, one began to believe in some kind of Masonic conspiracy, for the names of the same families recurred time and time again, and no fewer than five Presidents were commemorated as Grand Masters of Liberian Masonry. One began to understand the frustration that Liberians who were outside the magic circle of power and influence must have felt.

I left the Masonic building and went to the other end of the city, to that part of it which had once been the centre of official life and where many of the country's foremost institutions had been situated. Most of the buildings were erected in the 1960s, not a good decade for architecture, least of all in Africa, and most of them were now deserted. The Ministry of Foreign Affairs, a large, ten-storey slab in the style of Le Corbusier, looked as though an enormous and exceptionally rough party had taken place in it, and all the party goers had deserted it to nurse their hangovers, leaving the wreckage behind. The Temple of Justice was not, as the name might suggest, a neo-classical building, but another office block of great ugliness. It, too, was deserted, and many of its windows were smashed. On the concrete end of the block were some words written in huge metal letters:

LET JUSTICE BE DONE TO ALL MEN

But it was the University of Liberia nearby that I wanted to visit, the only university in the country and therefore an institution of the greatest significance in Liberia's life. It was

38

abandoned, deserted. On the edge of the campus lay the university's fleet of twenty or more buses, once used to transport the students, but now mere scrap metal, their wheels removed, their windows shot out, their bodywork rusting in the ferocious humidity of the coastal climate.

The campus itself was a collection of undistinguished yellow-painted buildings, most of them of only two floors, in pleasant grounds with flame trees and lawns which, for lack of attention, were fast becoming tangled and overgrown. Perfect silence reigned, but it was the silence of death rather than the monastic silence of study.

All the buildings were pock-marked by bullets. It was difficult to guess at what, if anything, the guns had been aimed, since every building, with the exception of the Harvey S. Firestone Science Building, had been equally affected. The latter, though, had been completely destroyed, reduced to rubble, probably by direct hits from rockets. There was irony in this (or justice, as certain hotheads might claim), for Firestone was the man who, more than any other, brought Liberia into the modern world. The liberal benefactor of the university, in 1926 he established a vast rubber plantation in Liberia to break the world monopoly of rubber supplies which the British then had, and which held the American automobile industry to ransom. Firestone is often regarded as having been an exploiter, for the wages on his plantation were not high; but in countries such as Liberia, one man's exploitation is another man's development, and conditions on the plantation were better than elsewhere in the country. Canny to the last, the Firestone Company sold its plantation to a Japanese competitor a few months before the outbreak of the civil war which destroyed it. And then the civil war destroyed Firestone's memorial at the university.

I walked into the administration block. The filing cabinets were still there, and a few tables, but no chairs. All the drawers of the filing cabinets had been pulled out as far as they would come, and the files were strewn on the floor. The tables were promiscuously piled with documents, and files were opened at random, as though illiterate men in a rage had attacked the offices and attempted to learn the secret of writing by scanning every page upon which they could clap their eyes.

One could not avoid stepping on documents, but such is my reverence for the written word that I felt somehow barbarous in doing so. To walk on someone's signature is like stepping, *in absentia*, on their fingers. If ever the university were to resume its work, it would take weeks of hard labour merely to restore the papers in just one of the rooms to some kind of order. I looked through a few papers at random: here an invitation to a professor to attend an academic conference at the University of Newcastle upon Tyne, there a decree by President Tolbert that such and such a university functionary should accompany him on an important state visit to Uganda. Regulations, timetables, requests for leave, complaints, appeals for help: the entire life of a complex institution was heedlessly laid bare by those with only hatred in their heart. By all accounts, it was followers of Samuel Doe who wrought the destruction of the University of Liberia.

Like many men of little education who suddenly find themselves in an exalted position, Doe demonstrated a marked ambivalence towards the world of learning. He hated it, yet craved its recognition. In Africa as nowhere else does the educated man make his feelings of superiority over the uneducated perfectly plain; it is evident in the very way a man who has learnt book, as they say in West Africa, speaks to an illiterate. Hence it is unlikely that Doe had never felt the lash of an educated man's tongue, had never felt the gnawing sense of inferiority that a man of uncertain educational attainments always feels in the presence of the professional and the lettered. When he came to power, he was soon surrounded by intellectuals, yet his English was halting and incorrect. He could never be sure they weren't laughing at him behind his back – the worst thing, next to a plot.

The way to a tyrant's heart is through a doctorate and in 1982 the South Koreans, anxious to gain access to Liberia's precious hardwoods, awarded him an honorary doctorate. Thereafter it became almost treasonable not to refer to him in public as 'Doctor' Doe. Nevertheless, he himself recognized the difference between a real degree and an honorary one; and he decided to enrol at the university as an undergraduate in political science.

Of course, he was not just any student. He could not spare the time to go to the university, so the university had to come to him. Among the papers on the floor of the administrative offices of the university, I found a glossy pamphlet entitled *The University of Liberia Reaches Out: Reflections*. Printed in 1989, it contains sycophantic essays by the academics who went to the Executive Mansion every evening for three years to teach the President. There are photographs in the pamphlet of the presidential student, hard at work in the Executive Mansion, a telephone on his desk, a microscope on the shelf behind him, or with his fellow-students (specially selected to study with him) in the classroom in the Mansion, looking like no other students, one of them dressed in a light silvery-grey suit, with matching emerald green silk tie and breast pocket handkerchief and the two-tone grey shoes of a gigolo.

Less than a year before his death, this is what they wrote about His Excellency:

On the whole, I would rate the President as a man not only of superior aptitude, initiative, with a sense of responsibility but also as a highly intelligent and sociable person, with an excellent emotional control and paternal concern for other people. The President's performance was obviously superior to that of each of the members of his class. Perhaps the difference was based on his superior aptitude, ability, devotion and natural inclination toward the pursuit of academic excellence.

I see the triangular union between Government – The President – The University of Liberia. In this union, with the President as its base, I perceive a future in which the Government, through the instrumentality of the Chief Architect, now a Political Scientist, may come to rely on the professional services [of] the University of Liberia . . . to facilitate the efficient and effective performance of the task of nation building.

It is with deep humility and profound gratitude to God and His Excellency Dr Samuel Kanyon Doe . . . that [I] write with joy and deep satisfaction the 'Foreword' Message to Reflections on the Special Academic Program.

Unsurprisingly, perhaps, Dr Doe graduated *Summa Cum Laude* with the highest marks ever recorded in the university – shortly before its total destruction.

I moved on to the Ibrahim Badamasi Babangida School of International Studies, pausing briefly to look at a notice-board to which photographs of smiling students on an exchange trip to Strasbourg were still affixed. The building

42

was destroyed and looted. Babangida was the military President of Nigeria, and inside the school named in his honour I found the programme, edged in red, white and blue, for the special convocation of the University of Liberia for the conferral upon him of a doctorate of laws, *honoris causa*, and for the official opening of the school, some twenty months before its destruction. On the cover was the university motto, *Lux in Tenebris*, Light in Darkness, and at the end of the programme were the words of two anthems, those of the University and of Liberia:

> *Lux in Tenebris*, O Alma Mater:
> To thee we lift our joyous lay;
> May thy benignant radiance far-spreading
> Lighten our years for aye . . .

And then the national anthem, to complete the irony:

> All hail Liberia, hail!
> All hail Liberia, hail!
> In union strong success is sure . . .

The furniture had been removed from the school, but in one of the rooms there was still a blackboard, and on it was written (in very bad French) a poignant little prayer dated 1 October 1990: 'The War is ending. There are too many material and human losses in this country. Why? Down with racism and sectarianism. Let us unite, my brothers and sisters, to build the country once more.' Underneath, in different handwriting, was an angry response: 'Please, when you come here do not write on this board.'

Who had written this? Some deranged caretaker, sent mad by the loss of the institution he loved, the Lear of the

43

university? What kind of mind was witness to the obliteration of an entire city, yet worried about writing on a blackboard?

I wanted to see the library. *En route*, I found a book lying abandoned in the grass, entitled *The Rational Manager*. The library was among the largest buildings on the campus, five storeys high. Its brickwork was peppered by bullet holes, and many of its windows were smashed, but the fabric was less damaged than that of most of the buildings in the university. It was locked, too late to have prevented many of its books from appearing for sale on the streets of the city. Later I found a bookseller whose wares, spread across the pavement, came exclusively from the university library. I had a sudden fit of morality, and refused to buy anything from him, pointing to the stamp of the university on the title pages. The bookseller was bemused by my outward show of fastidiousness: from where else, he asked, was he supposed to get his books? Besides, everything that was for sale in Monrovia was looted, the only difference being that with these books, one knew *where from*. Feeling foolish, I stuck to my resolution: I would only join in the looting if, like Pontius Pilate, I remained in ignorance of it.

The library had been the largest in the country (no larger, in fact, than an average municipal library at home), but was now in disarray. The chief librarian's office looked as though a jealous spouse had gone on the rampage through it, exacting retribution for a recently discovered love-affair. On a desk was a small paperback, its front cover burnt. I opened it to see what it was: *Fathers and Sons* by Turgenev. What would Ivan Sergeyevich, a man who valued civilization above all else, have made of this savagery? Would he have recognized in the book-burners of the world the lineal descendants of Bazarov himself? I do not think so; there was something more elemental, less cerebral, than his character Bazarov's nihilism at work here – a visceral hatred of the library and all it stood for, the revenge of the unschooled for all the slights and humiliations they had received at the hands, and tongues, of the schooled. And the impulse to destroy what you cannot understand is always a powerful one, waiting to be acted upon once the normal restraints of law and order are removed.

I walked through the three or four floors of the library. Books had been pulled from the shelves and hurled across the floor, and even the books that remained on the shelves were at strange angles, as though the destroyers had been interrupted in their work and obliged to flee in mid-vandalism. There were rooms piled five feet high in books, their subject matter promiscuously intermixed, soil science with Herodotus. The covers were bent or torn off, the pages ripped out. In humid tropical countries it is difficult enough to keep books in good condition: the covers curl, the black mould spreads, the cockroaches, the termites and the worms gnaw at paper and at bindings. But here they were piled as if in preparation for a bonfire, round which the illiterate and the doubtfully literate might dance for joy.

I left the university, repeatedly glancing over my shoulder at the devastation and the desertion, and I – who was not a Liberian – suddenly felt that unnameable but deep emotion that great music or great art evokes.

4

THE MATERNITY
HOSPITAL

But if the university was devastated, what word might one use to describe the nearby Maternity Hospital? It was a building painted turquoise (the previous government seemed to have favoured this colour), but now it had neither roof nor windows. The notice announcing visiting hours, planted in what had once been a lawn but was now a wilderness, was rotting away and was almost illegible. In the *porte-cochère* which had once received arriving patients, an ambulance stood, without wheels, engine or seats, a mere rusting shell.

The hospital was on a high piece of ground that sloped sharply down towards the river bank, and gave a view of the broad and lazy tea-brown stream winding through the jungle that I, at any rate, found enchanting and romantic, though the steamy heat that seemed to rise from below presaged horrible tropical fevers and discomforts. On the sloping ground, close to the river banks, was a small settlement of huts, too humble to have excited the interest of soldiers of any faction. People moved among the huts, carrying on their daily lives, washing, fetching wood, pounding cassava. The murmur of conversation and the sound of children's games rose indistinctly to the top of the bluff and, looking down, one might have thought that nothing untoward had ever

47

happened in the vicinity. The African had survived where the alien was destroyed.

Again, the destruction of the Maternity Hospital was not casual, the result of misdirected rocket or artillery fire: it was the product of labour, intense and systematic. The hospital had been dismantled, piece of equipment by piece of equipment, and then mutilated – in the manner of a psychopathic murderer who not only kills but dismembers his victims.

By the side of the hospital overlooking the river I found the records of hundreds of births that had taken place there. Charts recording the progress towards delivery – the mother's heart rate, her blood pressure, the frequency of her uterine contractions, the degree of dilatation of her cervix, the baby's heart rate – were scattered on the ground. Also to be found there were the records of infant welfare clinics, tracing the growth of babies over several months on a simple graph, alerting doctors and nurses to the onset of malnutrition or other disorders. These records were smeared with excrement: they were used now for lavatory paper.

I can't say for certain whether the people who used these records thus had any conception of what they were for, what they meant, or whether they had merely used the first paper that came to hand in a situation in which even lavatory paper had to be looted from somewhere or other. Yet I could not help feeling that this action was symbolic, and not the result of chance; for it was the medical records alone that had been used in this way, and not the other pieces of paper that abounded in the hospital.

I am a doctor, and though I have maintained a certain distance from my profession, the better to see it whole, and have sometimes mocked its absurder pretensions, I nevertheless regard the achievements of medical science as among Man's greatest triumphs. When one considers the effort it has taken for mankind to move from ignorance to partial knowledge of the diseases that have afflicted it immemorially, one must be moved. And so, when I saw what appeared to be a repudiation, a total rejection, of modern medical science, a literal shitting upon it, I was more than a little shocked. Could it be that, far from viewing such science as beneficent, the people of Liberia had long resented it as an alien imposition, and as soon as restraints were removed, demonstrated their real feelings towards it?

It is true, of course, that western principles and practices are not left unchanged in their translation to Africa. It is possible, indeed it is likely, that the clinics of the Maternity Hospital did not function in the manner described in textbooks, that the staff extorted bribes for doing what they were in any case supposed to do (salaries often arriving late or not at all), that there were shortages of basic medicines, that the poor were made to feel their impotence through the brusqueness with which they were treated. But I do not think this accounts for the hatred of the Maternity Hospital that its obliteration made plain to me. The sentiment went much deeper than that; it was elemental, like lava under the thin crust of the earth's surface, waiting to erupt from a volcano.

Nothing could have prepared me for the sight and stench that greeted me when I entered the hospital. I very nearly gagged. A ramp sloped upwards from a long dark corridor, from which several large rooms, once clinics, gave off. Human excrement covered the ground, together with growth charts, health education pamphlets, pills, broken pieces of equipment, syringes, bandages and other dressings. One or two obstetric chairs, their covers slashed, their

49

mechanisms destroyed, were to be seen, tipped over into the mess around them. On the ground I found some unfilled certificates:

MINISTRY OF HEALTH AND SOCIAL WELFARE

This certificate is issued to ...... in honor of the fact that he/she is

AN OUTSTANDING PARENT

Based on the fact that the child has been fully vaccinated

One of my main concerns was that I shouldn't get shit on my espadrilles.

My driver guided me through this mess as if he were a Sherpa in the Himalayas and I were a rich and whimsical tourist with no experience of mountain climbing. In fact, he had not been to the Maternity Hospital since its destruction, and I asked him, as we picked our way along the corridor, what he thought of what he saw and smelled. He said it was 'bad-o', and he shook his head in sorrow, but I thought this was a performance for my benefit rather than something deeply felt. He knew what I would think, and to please me said he thought the same. His manner was very different when he talked of the Krahn tribe or 'the late Doe': his eyes blazed then, and though I liked him a great deal, and came to rely upon him implicitly, I saw the light of future massacres in his eyes.

The truth was that I met only one Liberian who really cared about the destruction of institutions such as the Maternity Hospital, and he was Americo-Liberian. From the graphs, forms and educational pamphlets I found lying scattered in the deserted wards and out-patient clinics, it appeared to me that the hospital had once (and not so very long ago) been trying to do all the things recommended and required by aid workers to reduce the infant mortality rate and to improve the health of children; yet the completeness with which those efforts were now extinguished called into question the very assumptions on which they were based.

In a world such as ours in which magical thinking has been almost eliminated, in which religious belief, if any, has been pushed to the periphery of our existence, and interest in the supernatural is the province of the under-educated and the feeble-minded, it is self-evidently a good thing to reduce the infant mortality rate. Who could doubt the importance of saving human life? Indeed, what could be more important than to do so? But such a scale of values is not universal, and to people for whom every event, whether good or bad, has a supernatural meaning and explanation, there may be things of much greater importance. The death of an infant is not the ultimate disaster that it appears to be among us: rather, it is a symbol of something else, and is no less meaningful than survival itself.

An infant mortality rate is not like an elephant at a distance of twenty yards, something visible without training to everyone; nor is a society with an infant mortality rate of a hundred per thousand live births necessarily ten times unhappier than one with an infant mortality only a tenth as great. Yet missionaries for 'rational' values (by which, of course, we mean our own), spread the worship of the infant mortality rate around the globe with evangelical zeal. Before there can be progress, they believe, people must be taught dissatisfaction with their lot. Misery is the engine of history, and there is nothing quite like statistics for making people miserable.

Every cloud has its silver lining, however. The missionaries who bring the infant mortality rate also bring new four-wheel drive vehicles, Johnny Walker Black Label and renewed hope to prostitutes. African politicians are astute enough to realize that there are no free trips to Paris, Brussels or New York unless they pretend an interest in the things that seem to concern these earnest foreigners with a high standard of living; the infant mortality rate is a matter to which, like sin, no one can admit he is indifferent. And so begins the wearisome game of more-compassionate-than-thou.

Immunization programmes are instituted, not because they save lives, but because they bring in their wake training courses abroad and other perks. The aid workers are content in their salaries and in their awareness of doing good; the government is happy because it is able, whenever it is accused of corruption and of indifference to the welfare of the people, to point in refutation to the immunization programme; only the people themselves are discontented. They know the programme is a Trojan horse from which will spring government officials attempting new exactions. And they will be badgered to do things for their own good which they do not wish to do, and in whose efficacy they would prefer not to believe.

When you immunize a population whose conception of life is profoundly magico-religious, you are not carrying out a merely technical procedure: you are challenging its very conception of life. You are implying that all the propitiatory rites by which it previously sought to assuage the forces of death were useless, that its wise men were not wise at all, but fraudulent, and that its philosophy – or more exactly, its *Weltanschauung* – is false and childish. Measures that are ostensibly carried out for such a population's own good are therefore culturally disorientating; the former equilibria are destroyed, and old knowledge is discredited without new understanding to replace it. A situation arises, therefore, in which there is lip-service on the government side, and passive resistance on the people's side. As for the aid workers, their illusions are preserved by the prospect of a duller life at home.

Perhaps it wasn't so surprising, then, that the Maternity Hospital, with its well baby clinics, growth charts, immunization certificates and myriad other imported means of interference in the lives of people, should have excited such hatred. One of the explanations I heard for the unpopularity and eventual downfall of Tolbert was that, far from being inactive or inefficacious, he was forever trying to get people to *do* things that they had never done before, thereby implying that they were in some way deficient. The Maternity Hospital was a symbol of this mania for change, and its destruction a conservative reaction. At least, that is what I surmised.

A group of homeless people had taken refuge in the ruins of another part of the hospital. They ate only rice, which they received as a hand-out from relief organizations, and they cooked it over fires made of broken up furniture, doors and window frames. They lived in rooms partitioned off by pieces of cloth suspended by wires; in contrast to the unimaginably filthy corridors, their living space was immaculately clean, and they had gathered, or looted, enough possessions and ornaments to give the space some feeling of domesticity. The ornaments were purest kitsch: large plastic flowers of lurid colour, or cheap Venetian gondola music boxes with plastic ballerinas at the prow; yet, in the circumstances, there was something moving about this attempt to reach beyond the realm of mere survival.

The inhabitants of the hospital were Krahn, members of the late Doe's tribe. I was told – by non-Krahn, of course – that Doe had armed every member of his tribe in Monrovia in an attempt to preserve his power, and that all the Krahn had been incorporated into the Armed Forces of Liberia. There was therefore no such man as an innocent Krahn, for the army had committed atrocity after atrocity. What degree of truth there was in this I cannot say. Even if all the Krahn *had* been soldiers in the army, would the concept of collective guilt have any moral validity? Was it not just another twist in the spiral of violence, an anticipatory excuse for genocide to come?

At any rate, it was obvious that the Krahn living in the hospital were frightened men. They were highly suspicious of us to begin with. The first little group to whom I spoke were monosyllabic in their answers, and haunted in their look; they had the darting, feral movements of hunted animals. They were short in stature and gave me the impression of having emerged recently from a dark forest; they appeared to be under the control of one of their number, a slightly taller individual incongruously dressed in a green velvet smoking jacket who carried a black attaché case. His eyes had a peculiar and chilling deadness that I came soon to recognize in Liberia. I cannot explain it, for the reflection of light from the cornea presumably obeys impersonal physical laws: the fact is, however, that the eyes of people such as he refused to shine, or to convey any information about the state of their owner's emotions, and if the eyes are the window of the soul, his were most decidedly a one-way window. He claimed at first to be a construction worker, his attaché case purportedly containing contracts for rebuilding work, but he later admitted that he was a lieutenant in the Armed Forces of Liberia. The fact that he had lied added considerably to the sinister impression he made. The only information I gleaned from his group – for such I concluded they were – was the meagre content of their diet, plain boiled rice. To prove it, a woman with pendulous shrivelled breasts showed me an iron bowl in which the rice had been boiled, the glutinous grains sticking to the metal, from which eager fingers of children tried hungrily to dislodge them.

Living in yet another part of the hospital, there was a group of six Krahn men who proved far less hostile towards me. Perhaps the difference is explicable by the absence when I was with them of my driver, who was a Mano from Nimba County, the very tribe which the Krahn now feared would massacre them if it had the chance. The six Krahn were not only willing to talk, but almost pathetically anxious to do so, and their words tumbled out of their mouths like something spilled. No one, it seemed, had ever asked them for their side of the story. One of them wore a T-shirt with a picture of the late Doe on it. Around the picture were printed some words: 'Congratulations to President Samuel K. Doe on the Tenth Anniversary of His Assumption of Power, April 12th 1990.' Less than six months later, of course, he was dead.

They told me that they were virtual prisoners in the Maternity Hospital. If they strayed more than a few hundred yards from the building, it was unlikely they would ever return alive. Certainly it was impossible for them to go to the part of the city where I stayed: they would be killed at once by the Gio or Mano. But how, I asked, would anyone know that they were Krahn? Was it written on their faces, did they carry distinctive tribal marks?

No, they said, it was nothing like that. Rather, the Krahn and the Gio and Mano had lived peacefully in Monrovia as neighbours before the civil war, and had never felt the slightest enmity. Indeed, many Krahn were married to Gio or Mano women, or were the offspring of such mixed marriages (tribal affiliation was determined by one's father's tribe). Having lived so amicably together, therefore, in such close proximity, everyone knew everyone else's tribe, for there had been neither means nor need to hide it. So if any Krahn entered a part of the city where there were Gio or Mano, he would be recognized immediately for what he was, and then killed. Freshly decapitated bodies of Krahn who had strayed too far were found every morning.

What, I asked, had brought about this terrible state of enmity between the tribes? The six of them grew excited, and all started to speak at once. Whatever else the civil war may have done, it had aroused and maintained a high level of interest in public affairs. I chose one of the six to speak on their behalf.

He explained that when Doe had come to power, 'the Congo people' (the Americo-Liberians) 'can not agree for that.' Until Doe's coup, 'they were enjoying'; that is to say, they ruled the roost, with all the attendant advantages of doing so. After Doe drove them out, they set about plotting his downfall, to which end they turned the Gio and Mano people against the Krahn. The Congo people were still the puppet-masters, the tribesmen still the puppets. Was not Taylor a Congo man?

There was no reason, then, why the Gio and Mano should have hated Doe and his government?

No. Only the Congo people made them hate it.

I liked these Krahn and wanted to believe what they said, though of course I couldn't. They appeared gentle, unlike the lieutenant in the green velvet jacket, and they were astonishingly courteous and trusting for people under constant and imminent threat of death. But even if the inter-tribal hatred had had the origins they ascribed to it, there were few grounds for optimism. What kind of people could

56

have been so easily manipulated into murderous, genocidal but groundless hatred? Would one wish to live in a country where such people were one's enemies?

One of the Krahn said he had something he wished to show me, and disappeared to his quarters. He returned with a paperback book with a shiny purple cover. It was entitled *Liberia: A Promise Betrayed*, and it was published in New York in 1986 by the Lawyers' Committee For Human Rights. Its owner treated it reverently, almost like a holy book; and later, when I tried to obtain it for myself in Liberia, I was told that no one who possessed a copy would willingly part with it. And as with a holy book, people derived whatever lessons they liked from it.

The owner of *Liberia: A Promise Betrayed* opened it to a preselected page – in fact, it had been opened so many times to this page that the book would have fallen open at it of its own accord. A sentence had been underlined in pencil, and he asked me to read it.

> A Gio scholar from Nimba County . . . put it this way: 'I'm afraid,' he said, 'that if they allow this man [Doe] to be killed, it will be recorded in history that there was once a tribe called Krahn in Liberia.'

As I did so, he smiled almost in triumph, the triumph of a man who has successfully proved a geometric theorem. True, the prediction was not a happy one, for it applied to him, his family and friends, announcing their imminent extinction; but at least it had the merit of accuracy, and there was lugubrious satisfaction in that. I suspect also that the evidence of foreign publications concerning themselves with the fate of the Krahn – with *his* fate, therefore – was a matter of pride to him.

57

The underlined passage in the book raised two questions, which I asked the six men. First, what had Doe done that his removal should lead to the annihilation of his tribe? And second, was there anything that could be done about it?

The jealousy of the other tribes was the answer to the first question. Doe had done nothing, but the other tribes were consumed by envy and a consequent thirst for revenge, which could be assuaged only by rivers of Krahn blood. As to the second question, they replied with a question of their own. *Why had the Americans not intervened?* They asked me this accusingly, as if I were responsible for the policy of the United States government. They told me that when two hundred marines landed at one point in the civil war, the Liberians thought they were saved. They did not realize at first that the marines came only to rescue foreigners, not to rescue them. But why not, when it would have been so easy for them? Were Liberians not men, worthy of salvation? Five hundred marines would have sufficed, fewer perhaps, to put an end to the war. Inevitably, they compared the efforts the Americans made on behalf of Kuwait with their studied indifference towards the far greater Liberian tragedy.

As often seems to happen to me when I am on distant shores, I found myself explaining American policy and, because I am by nature a controversialist, defending it. There were several reasons for the American inaction, I said. America loomed so large in the politics and culture of Liberia, that Liberians tended to assume the interest was reciprocated. Alas, this was not so. America was important to Liberia but Liberia was not important to America. Such interests as the Americans once had in the country were now gone: the rubber plantation was sold, the iron ore mines defunct, and Liberia's strategic importance destroyed by

58

new technology. As for purely humanitarian considerations, no one in the rest of the world would have believed in them, had the Americans intervened. On the contrary, they would have ascribed to the Great Satan the most sordid of selfish motives. And once the Americans had put a stop to the war, what would they have done next? A democratic government installed by them would have been open to nationalist accusations of betrayal; and all such a government's inevitable vices, from corruption to brutality, would have been blamed on the Americans, as if Liberians had never discovered for themselves how to offer and accept bribes, or to torture people to death. Since they had no vital interests at stake, it was wiser for the Americans to steer clear of Liberia.

It is not a comforting thought that one's travails, however terrible, are of no fundamental concern to others, but I have never subscribed to the view, commonly held in practice by liberals, that Africans, because of the historical wrongs done to them, should be protected from the truth as one sees it, either about themselves or about others; that the correct way to speak to them is in euphemisms; and that they deserve our self-censorship. The impulse to make allowances for other people may start out with humanitarian intentions, but it often ends up by degrading such people to something less than fully human: making allowances is an Olympian attitude, and one does not make allowances for one's equals. There are no doubt times when people ought to be spared the truth, but not, surely, when lack of realism may cost them their lives.

The six Krahn were anxious to show me round their little quarter of the hospital. On one side of the entrance to a corridor was a slogan painted by the Executive Mansion Guard who, the Krahn told me, had once occupied the building.

ARMED FORCES OF LIBERIA: SOLDIERS IN CHRIST

I was later to see the site of one of their pious massacres.

On the other side of the entrance was another message, somewhat less elevated in tone:

NO WATER IN THE BATHROOM SO DO NOT PUPU THERE
PLEASE,
I BEG YOU. THING ABOUT HUMAN AND LET BE GENT.

We went through a large tiled room, once a clinic. Pills crunched underfoot: they were antibiotics, for lack of which someone somewhere in the city was almost certainly dying of a simple disease at that very moment. On the wall was a copy of a letter, sent by a leper on the occasion of her graduation from the university, thanking the staff for having treated her so that she might continue her studies. Also on the wall was a health education poster in French about AIDS. It came from Mauritius and showed a man thrusting himself forward happily towards the welcoming embraces of several smiling young ladies, almost bare except for G-strings and stars upon their nipples.

LE SIDA
EVITEZ LES PARTENAIRES FACILES

I know that AIDS threatens the whole of the human race yet, in Liberian circumstances, there was something false about the stated concern (in a foreign language) over the epidemic. This health education propaganda was posted, I surmised, not from any genuine appreciation of the seriousness of the situation, but to satisfy foreign experts and aid donors that something was being done: for something, whatever it may be, is always better than nothing.

The owner of *Liberia: A Promise Betrayed* wanted to show me his little cache of books. He said he had rescued them, but I did not ask from where. He said he was preserving them against the day when Liberians might once more find them useful. He kept them on a little shelf in the corner of the building he had partitioned off as his bedroom, and upon which he, too, had tried to stamp his own personality. I copied down the titles: *Income Tax Workbook*, *Revolution Industrielle et Sous-developpement*, *The Autobiography of Haile Selassie*, *The Nature of Capital and Income*, *Fundamentals of Counselling*.

'Have you read them all?' I asked, wondering what kind of muddle so eclectic a collection would produce in his mind.

'Oh, no,' he said. 'I am only keeping them.'

He evidently revered books, whatever their content. This was no doubt a highly civilized attitude; but, as he waved goodbye to me and thanked me for coming to the Maternity Hospital, a question recurred to me that I had wanted to ask him at the outset. What did *you* do during the war?

5

THE ALL-LIBERIA
CONFERENCE

I was woken on my second morning in Monrovia, as I had been on my first, by the news on the BBC World Service played very loud, possibly as a public service, by a vendor of cigarettes (who regularly hoped I had taken up smoking in the intervals between the many times I passed him) outside Stouffer's Bar. The news, of course, was terrible: war, genocide, famine, epidemic, riot, and economic collapse; but there was something reassuring about the calm, clear and measured way in which it was all related. Dictators may rise and fall, but BBC announcers go on for ever.

It is astonishing how, in many parts of Africa, people listen to the BBC to find out what is really happening three miles away. The BBC is their standard of truth, against which rumour and supposition are measured. On my second day in Monrovia, I had the good fortune to meet the BBC's correspondent there.

He was a young American called Scott Stearns and he was the only correspondent who had lived in Liberia throughout the civil war. He was twenty-four years old and very ambitious; in choosing Liberia, he had shown not only courage but considerable shrewdness. He had seen a great deal – more and worse than most of us will see in a lifetime – and his months in Monrovia would be sufficient to convince future editors that he was tough enough to stand any assignment. His career had got off to an auspicious start.

Scott had fair, curly hair and sky-blue eyes, which made him extra-conspicuous in Monrovia. He had that intense stare and nervous manner of scanning the horizon common to all newshounds. There were stringers from Reuters and Agence France Presse in town, and he could not afford to miss anything of importance. One rarely had his undivided attention, and I confess I thought of *Scoop* every time I met him.

He told me that I had arrived at a most fortunate time, because the All-Liberian Conference was convening to settle the war that very day at the Unity Conference Center. I was welcome to come along. He was leaving in a few minutes. I was too cowardly in the face of his reporter's eagerness to tell him of my scepticism about Historic Moments, of which the All-Liberia Conference was supposedly one. In my experience, HMs are not all they are cracked up to be; the moment tends to drag out into days or even weeks, having been postponed several times, until one is not quite sure when exactly it occurred, or whether it has occurred at all. Nevertheless, I jumped into his Volkswagen Kombi with its BBC sticker on the windscreen, and we started out for the Unity Conference Center.

Fuel was so expensive in Monrovia, and so intermittently available, that Scott coasted down the hill. 'Yesterday I reached the mosque,' he said, but today we were less lucky. Scott had to engage the gears a hundred yards before we reached the grey breeze-block mosque, which was so raw and ugly that one could not make out whether it was in the process of construction or destruction.

En route to the Center, Scott talked passionately of Liberian politics. I understood his passion: after only a few hours in Monrovia, it was as if nowhere else in the world existed for me, and Scott had been there nearly a year. Alas, I couldn't follow all that he said because the names of local politicians, who loomed so large in his daily life, meant nothing to me. I did not interrupt his flow, however, to ask him questions, because I was ashamed to admit that I had arrived in a place so difficult to reach with so little preparation: I had read the book by Graham Greene's cousin Barbara Greene, about her trek with the novelist through the Liberian jungle in 1935, and that was all.

We were stopped from time to time by the ECOMOG road-blocks, but the soldiers knew Scott and never gave us any trouble, only occasionally asking to see the inside of our glove compartment – in which, for some reason, was secreted a tin of ladies' fingers (or okra) in tomato sauce. Later I observed that the middle of the day was a good time to travel if you wanted to avoid molestation at the road-blocks, because it was then too hot for security, and the soldiers would languidly wave you through from under the shade of a tree.

We arrived at the Center, some few miles out of town. It was part of one of those complexes, called in West Africa 'ultra-modern', built for the 1979 meeting of the Organization of African Unity at a cost of $200,000,000, which mysteriously prove so difficult to maintain once the captains and the kings have departed. True to form, it had no electricity or water, and the lavatories were ultra-something-else, but in the car park were the remains of the *sine qua non* of present-day African government, a fleet of black Mercedes. The cars had not escaped the civil war undamaged, however; many of them had been badly dented, and others had polythene to replace glass where the windows had been shot out.

65

Although we arrived just as the meeting was scheduled to begin, the ultra-modern entrance hall was nearly empty. A few of the delegates stood around, quietly talking to one another: Scott groaned. He had come out there every day for the last ten days, under the illusion that something historic, or at least newsworthy, was going to happen. An atmosphere of inspissated inertia had descended upon the building, through which one moved as though opposed by powerful magnetic forces. I knew at once that we were destined to spend long hours there, fearing to leave but longing to go.

I was approached by a man in a brown velvet jacket with a pipe in his mouth and a sheaf of papers under his arm. He was a delegate, who was taking advantage of the recess in the conference to sell his poems. He made for me with the precision of a Tomahawk missile.

I bought a copy for five Liberian dollars. It consisted of a dozen stencilled pages, stapled together. The collection was titled *Civil War and Peace*, and there was an epigraph in brackets underneath the large letters of the title:

(The Liberian Civil War must end to glorify Wisdom in this
Land of Freedom and Liberia: O Sweet Liberia
Stop Weeping.)
By:
C. Plato Warner, Sr.
A Liberian Poet/Writer

Underneath the list of contents, there was a notice to readers:

If you want to contact the Poet/Writer for any writing

66

contract, please inform the NATIONAL CONGRESS FOR
UNITY AND PEACE IN LIBERIA (NACUP), U.N. Drive,
Antoinette Tubman Stadium (in care of).

Commonly known as "PEACE AMBASSADORS."

I glanced briefly at the poems, and decided to save
detailed examination for later. C. Plato Warner, poet,
novelist, politician and Chief Inspector for the Department
of Sewage and Water (currently in abeyance), was delighted
to talk to a fellow-writer. He had six full novels in the
drawer of his desk, he said, still in manuscript form for lack
of publishers in Liberia. What were they about, I asked?
Politics, he replied. He was, he added, particularly interested in the moral aspect of politics.

I asked him for his views on the Liberian situation, and he
told me he was a Doe man himself, though he admitted that
the late Doe (as he is almost always called in Liberia, just as
Tubman and Tolbert are called the late Tubman and the late
Tolbert) was perhaps led astray by bad advisors, not having
been an educated man. Later, I noticed C. Plato Warner in
the company of the present leaders of Doe's political party,
former Vice-President Harry Moniba and ex-Minister Bai
Gbala, villains if ever I saw them, and I wondered how
association with the inheritors of Doe's monstrous tribalistic
legacy could be reconciled with the words of his Preface to
his poems:

All the falsehoods of proudness, hatred, arrogance, stub-
borness and revenge must go. The false notion that
certain class in Liberia has a leadership 'PURITY' over
others must go. The false notion that certain people are in
fact better than others in Liberia must also go. Ethnic and
tribal strife must go. The cruel vices of greed, anger,

murder and selfishness or deceit must go. The mental slavery of good-fornothing arguments that keep this country to be isolated from the rest of the civilized world must go.

These are the fine sentiments of our national pride and culture which are being creatively expressed in Poetry in this short collection of revolutionary POEMS . . .

The tenor of his revolutionary poems (in which 'beautiful armless ladies', victims apparently of the war, make several appearances) may be accurately gauged by the first two stanzas of the ode 'ECOMOG Is Beautiful':

ECOMOG is a beautiful organization
That is why Liberians must prove a revelation
    Of wisdom to deliver Peace at the All-Liberian
            Conference
    To bring pride and dignity to our African Brothers
            and sisters.

    ECOMOG has beautiful soldiers with their smiling
            faces
    They handle each by professional discipline the
            cases
Of robbery and looting by simple Liberians
Never mind! Peace is all we want.

Poor C. Plato Warner, dreaming of literary fame and glory. I was told that he carried his pipe purely for effect, that he never actually smoked it. He believed, apparently, that all poets smoked pipes.

When it became clear that history was not going to be made before lunch, Scott suggested that we go to the nearby Hotel Africa, where lunch was served, free of charge, to all the delegates, observers and journalists at the conference.

'So there is such a thing as a free lunch after all,' I said. 'Although it's a long way to come for it.'

The Hotel Africa was part of the Unity Conference Center complex. The heads of state had their own villas in the grounds nearby, filled with champagne and whisky; their aides and hangers-on were relegated to the hotel, designed in the OAU–Las Vegas style. By comparison with the taste of modern African despots, that of King Farouk was restrained and understated. Of course there was no electricity or fresh water in the Hotel Africa: the only water to wash in was sea water and the only water to drink was mineral water imported from France. The hotel had been built on the presumption of air conditioning, in the absence of which the rooms became unbearably stuffy and mouldy. The sea breezes were rigorously excluded by sealed windows: sea breezes are not ultra-modern.

Lunch was in the casino, converted into a restaurant. The casino was a vast room with a low ceiling covered entirely in polished brass. Even without lighting, in semi-darkness in the middle of a tropical day, it gave the impression of ineffable vulgarity. Was it for access to places such as this that the first generation of African despots tyrannized their people? I think it was. As I looked around, a single thought ran through my mind: 'At least Louis XIV built Versailles.'

The delegates sat around the tables, deep in political discussion. Lunch was delayed by an hour and a half. When finally the food arrived, there was a scramble for it as desperate as the scramble in which I had participated at Lagos Airport once the boarding of the aircraft was announced (the Togolese market women had brushed me contemptuously aside with their baskets, seemingly laden with lead ingots). The leaders of the nation were terrified that there would not be enough lunch for them.

It was in the casino that I met Dr Togba-Nah Tipoteh, the author of a little book called *Democracy: The Call of the Liberian People*. I had bought it on the street the night before, and I had already read it. Dr Tipoteh was himself a Man of the People, and was leader of an organization called MOJA, the Movement for Justice in Africa. (It was no coincidence that *moja* means unity in Swahili, for one of MOJA's slogans was *Uhuru na Moja*, Freedom and Unity – the national motto of Tanzania, where there is neither freedom nor unity.) Dr Tipoteh was dressed in West African costume, which is much more suited to the humid climate than our close-fitting clothes, and had already undergone that physical expansion which is the mark of a man of consequence in Africa. His skin glistened with health and well-being.

Dr Tipoteh's little book had been banned in Liberia for several years, and the author, to whom I introduced myself as a journalist, inscribed it 'In the Struggle for Freedom of the Press'. He had been Budget Adviser to the Government of Liberia from 1971 to 1973 and the first Minister of Planning and Economic Affairs in Doe's government, until Doe suspected him of plotting a coup, whereupon he went into exile in Ghana and Holland, from which he had only recently returned.

The book, written in 1981, is an indictment of the Tolbert government, and indeed of the whole Americo-Liberian heritage. To illustrate the point, there is a photograph on page sixteen of Tubman and Tolbert standing outdoors, with palm trees in the background, in full evening dress in the middle of the day, the left breasts of their tailcoats covered in decorations, sashes across their dress shirts, their silk top hats placed over their hearts as the national anthem is played and the military brass stand rigidly to attention behind them, all salutes and gold braid. It is absurd but, to anyone who knows the Liberian climate, heroically absurd.

Not surprisingly, Dr Tipoteh sees neither the comic nor the heroic, but only the lamentable, aspect of the scene. He gives the picture the following caption:

Tubman and Tolbert in Tails
Which Way Liberia?
Americo-European or African?

In the text he enumerates the deficiencies of the *ancien régime*. It was corrupt, oppressive, and culturally inauthentic, he says; he makes much of the fact that the radio station announced programmes of African music with the words 'And now it is time for African music', but never announced any programme with the words 'And now it is time for American music', as though Liberia were not in Africa and African music were played only for ethnographic interest.

Reading and meeting Dr Tipoteh made me realize at once the profundity and importance of the injunction above the entrance to the Academy in ancient Athens: Know Thyself. Dr Tipoteh did not know himself. He might have raged against cultural mongrelization, but he was a cultural mongrel himself (perhaps that is why he raged so). I was told by a school friend of his that his 'real' name, or the name with which he was born, was Rudolf Roberts; he changed it to Togbah-Nah Tipoteh as part of a personal back-to-Africa movement. The name he chose, Togbah-Nah, which means 'Bringer of the Message' in the Kru language, is hardly the name of one who wishes to melt anonymously into the crowd of the downtrodden, to absorb its culture and become one with it. Dr Tipoteh wanted justice for all, but only if he were the one to bring it about.

71

His book, completed before Doe turned savage and before he had to flee for his life, displays no awareness that things might get worse rather than better; in his limited imagination, the *ancien régime* is already the worst imaginable, the grievances against it so grave that anything that comes after it must be an improvement. As usual in such tracts, there is no acknowledgement of the intrinsic difficulties facing a country such as Liberia: if there is poverty, someone is to blame for it and must therefore be eliminated. There is no awareness, not the faintest inkling, of deeper forces at work in the country than an intellectual adherence to the Enlightenment values of freedom, justice and democracy; no mention of the greed that gnawed at the hearts of the revolutionaries, and was soon to devastate the country, nor of the depth of the tribal feeling that was about to be unleashed. It was not only of himself that Dr Tipoteh was ignorant; his academic training had deprived him of knowledge of everyone else as well.

Poor Dr Tipoteh! His political superego told him that all men are equal, but his personal *id* told him that he was a leader of men. So he was an élitist in everything except his opinions. When I met him, I asked him for the new Preface he had written to his book. After the 1980 coup, things had not worked out quite as he had hoped or, more culpably, expected. He kindly gave me the Preface, a single sheet of paper, and also a large photograph of himself: in my experience, the few people who genuinely believe in the equality of man do not carry photographs of themselves in their attaché cases for distribution to as many people as possible.

The revised Preface was written in March 1990, in The Hague. There is no admission that his inflammatory and wildly unrealistic teachings may have played some part in the evolution of the disaster; much less is there a *mea culpa* for his lack of prescience in precisely the area of his supposed expertise. On the contrary: having stuck his neck out once before, and having had his head (only just metaphorically) cut off, he returns willingly to the execution block of political prophecy: 'At the launching of the Revised Preface, the people of Liberia are beginning to seize the initiative by exerting pressures geared towards the removal of the Doe regime and the installation of democracy in the Liberian society.' These words were written but a few months before the destruction of Monrovia and the transformation of half the population of the country into refugees.

I saw Dr Tipoteh once more, at a rally to commemorate the eighteenth anniversary of the founding of MOJA. It was held in a basketball court in the centre of Monrovia. On one side of the court sat Dr Tipoteh; on the other, the disciplined ranks of his humble supporters, who occasionally were encouraged by a chorus master to chant, in impressive if frightening unison, slogans about freedom and democracy.

Dr Tipoteh sat impassively throughout the welcoming dances performed by a group of women to the accompaniment of songs rhetorically exalting justice, political struggle and the Mother Continent of Africa. Here in the dancing was the culture which Dr Tipoteh so extolled in his book (and the study of which he wished to make compulsory in Liberian schools), yet he did not share the evident enthusiasm of the crowd and had an expression almost of disdain on his face, as if the monotonous rhythms of the music were all very well for people of little education, but not for those with doctorates of philosophy. His manner of sitting, more indicative of his true beliefs than any words he could utter,

73

turned his chair into a chiefly throne.

His speech, which was long and dull, was the main event of the afternoon. He was introduced to the crowd by a lady who recited the positions he had held (excluding those in the Doe government), the same list as appeared on the back of the photograph he had handed me with the Revised Preface:

Senior United Nations Advisor, AAU/ECA/UNDP Africa Economic Recovery and Development Program.

United Nations Consultant on Security, Stability, and Development in Africa (SSCDA).

Member, United Nations International Advisory Board on Structural Adjustment in Africa.

Member, Consultative Group on Economic Integration in West Africa.

I suspect that Dr Tipoteh would have been furious had he not been introduced to his followers in this manner, followers to whom the list of positions he had held must have conveyed little except inchoate visions of chauffeur-driven Mercedes in American and European cities, and banquets with people of world importance: enough, however, to give him that aura of living on a completely different plane which every aspiring charismatic leader of the masses needs.

A man of the people who sits like a king; an intellectual who changes his name to recapture his African authenticity, and then appends an academic title to it. Of such confusions was catastrophe wrought. As in so much of Africa, thought, sentiment and ambition in Liberia were not conjoined; the result was an all too potent brew of liberal rhetoric and atavistic feeling which destroyed the country.

6

THE PEACE SETTLEMENT

At last the Historic Moment arrived. One might have been
forgiven for thinking that the *really* historic moment occurred when the electricity was, briefly, restored to the conference centre, and that the actual conference to settle the civil
war was merely an epiphenomenon. At any rate the delegates, informed by some mysterious means of the restora-
tion of the electricity supply and hence of the air conditioning, started to return in large numbers to the hall. Suits,
lounge and safari, mingled with Mandingo boubous, the
long West African robes; Dr Tipoteh wore something
between a Mao and a Mobutu costume.

It had been a lengthy and tedious wait, enlivened only by
the spread of rumour and a BBC World Service news
programme, *Focus on Africa*, with reports from all over the
continent. Scott had with him a small but powerful radio,
and a little crowd of delegates gathered round to hear the
latest news. The first item caused quite a stir. In Benin, the
formerly Marxist President, Mathieu Kerekou, who had cut
down the trees along the streets of the capital, Cotonou,
because he said they were symbolic of French colonial rule,
had acceded to demands for an election, which he had then
lost by a wide margin to his opponent, the Prime Minister,
Misoufu Soglo. The matter, however, had not ended there:

Soglo had, immediately on winning the election, contracted typhoid and been obliged to go to France for treatment. The rumour circulating in Cotonou was that Kerekou had caused Soglo's illness by putting ju-ju on him. I laughed, but then I saw that the faces around me, listening intently to the radio, were not smiling. They took the rumour very seriously; in a world of magic and meaning, such as they inhabited, there are no coincidences.

Of the lavatories in the conference centre I shall say nothing, except that in the dark, and without electric light, one could still find them, guided by senses other than sight. The conference hall itself was like such halls the world over: the architecture, the furnishings, the layout, the public address system, all conduced to the utterance of platitude. We entered it at long last. Scott was excited by the latest rumour: the head of Charles Taylor's delegation to the conference, Dr McDonald, had not returned from Gbarnga, Taylor's headquarters, whither he had gone to receive instructions from his leader about the response he was to make to a new set of proposals by the Interim Government of National Unity. Scott considered Dr McDonald's non-reappearance at the conference as a certain augury of his death, since to fall out of Taylor's favour while you were within his power was unhealthy in the extreme. In the event, it transpired that Dr McDonald had simply defected to the Interim Government's side.

The chairman of the conference, a bishop in a faeculant brown floral costume, sat under a large slogan sewn on to a sheet:

MONROVIA WELCOMES
YOU TO THIS ALL IMPORTANT
CONFERENCE

76

The sheet, however, had come unstuck and folded over onto itself, obscuring half the words of the slogan. For some reason this irritated me: I wanted to rush down and hang it straight (I cannot stand untidiness except in my own room). Whenever anyone uttered the words 'Our beloved homeland' – words which produce an almost physical revulsion in me, whoever uses them – I felt I wanted to shout out, 'Yes, but do you love it enough to put that sheet straight?' Because it was so easy a thing to get right, I took the failure to do so as an ill-omen for Liberia.

The bishop announced that the session would commence with an invocation. A woman preacher stepped forward and began her prayer. The public address system worked perfectly: it made what she said almost entirely incomprehensible. One received only a vague intimation of piety, and at one point I thought I heard her describe the struggle between two Biblical peoples, the Panamites and the Parasites. She grew emotional and a sob entered her voice. Just as she was about to lose control, however, she gave place to a solemn mullah, who was much in favour of peace and wisdom.

The floor was given to the new leader of Charles Taylor's delegation. Taylor himself had refused to attend the conference after at first having agreed to do so because he claimed – not unrealistically, in view of the number of enemies he had made – that his personal safety could not be guaranteed in Monrovia. It was universally agreed that Taylor had no intention of compromising with the assembled politicians who, though divided among themselves, were united against him.

I looked down on the conference from the press gallery. The delegates leant back in their comfortable executive chairs. Except for the complexion of the participants, the

77

scene reminded me irresistibly of the conference of *Sajudis*, the Lithuanian national movement, which I had attended in Vilnius three years earlier. The Lithuanians had just recovered the right to fly their national flag and sing their national anthem after nearly half a century of suppression; emotions were running high. I recalled the midnight marches of that time, attended by the entire population of the city, if not the country, and the spontaneous applause that broke out at the first public mention of the name of Lithuania's pre-war dictator; I remembered the joy which greeted the announcement by the leader of Lithuania's Communist Party that Vilnius Cathedral would henceforth be returned to religious use after decades as an art gallery and a concert hall, in which the seats had been turned away from the altar. But memory is a strange faculty: its priorities are not those of the conscious mind. The distinctly unhistoric moment that came back most clearly was the call for the establishment of more wayside shrines, made by a peasant woman in traditional costume. There was enthusiastic applause; behind me, observing the conference, sat the assembled Politburo of the Lithuanian Communist Party, their grey faces immobile from decades of emotionlessness and overeating. But now, uncertain of their power, they too applauded, though woodenly, as if the establishment of wayside shrines had always been part of the political programme of the Lithuanian Communist Party.

The leader of Taylor's delegation repeated Taylor's main objection to the conference: that it represented only Monrovia and not the whole of Liberia. This was an old complaint: that Monrovia and its adjacent county, Montserrado, unfairly dominated the political life of Liberia. But Taylor's demand that there should be a much larger number of delegates at the conference from outside Monrovia was at least as self-seeking as the rejection of his demand, since he would control completely the selection of the delegates from the territory he and his movement governed (insofar as that territory was not given over entirely to anarchy). It was not a question of democracy, but of power.

At first Taylor's man spoke in measured tones, but gradually the enormity of the injustice perpetrated by the rest of the delegates began to weigh upon him, and he grew shriller. Taylor's reasonable proposals had been turned down by these old political hacks who, now that Doe was dead, had crawled out of the woodwork (he had a point there). He conjured himself into a rage; in summary, there was no point, he said, in continuing with this farcical, unrepresentative and undemocratic conference which did not answer the aspirations of the Liberian people. With these words, the rest of his delegation walked out of the hall, as in the good old days at the United Nations, and he remained behind only a short while longer, to receive the jeers, boos and sarcastic applause of the remaining delegates.

It was announced (through the grapevine) that the leader of Taylor's delegation would immediately hold a press conference in the entrance hall, and all the reporters, mostly from the ill-printed and often virtually illegible news-sheets that had sprung up in Monrovia since the cease-fire, rushed out in a herd, carrying me with them. What was I going to do with the news I gathered? I had no means of communicating it to anyone, and in any case no one to whom it would have been of the slightest interest. As I stampeded with the herd, however, the important thing seemed to be the process, not the outcome. The leader of Taylor's delegation stood on a dais and said that he would read out a prepared statement, and would then leave without answering questions. There were disgruntled murmurs among the journalists, which he savoured : to disoblige with impunity is one of the pleasures of power.

His statement was merely a reiteration of what he had said in the conference hall, which itself had been said *ad nauseam* to those who had been in Liberia longer than I. He fairly trembled with outrage. If he was acting, he was an excellent actor: but I suspect that, while he spoke, he truly felt the emotion he displayed. He was bogus and sincere at the same time, a living example of the complexity of the human psyche. Surely he knew, at one level of cerebration or another, that his boss was a megalomaniac intent on power for its own sake, and that he himself was an opportunistic hanger-on? Yet he spoke in the language of the purest political philosophy, as if what mattered was the inviolability of human rights, rather than power and bank accounts. When he finished speaking, the reporters rushed forward and raised their hands to attract his attention to the questions they asked: did this mean the war would start up again, that the National Patriotic Front would henceforth attack ECOMOG soldiers, and that Charles Taylor would march on Monrovia? The leader of the delegation angrily refused to answer any such questions, as if his refusal, too, were an important matter of principle rather than a wholly arbitrary decision on his part. He strode towards the car (a large new Volvo with plywood replacing the bullet damaged rear window) which was waiting to take him back to Taylor territory. The junior members of his delegation had been rather less successful in fending off the questions of the reporters and had become involved in acrimonious exchanges of opinion, but eventually they broke free and climbed into the lesser vehicles that followed their chief's Volvo.

The historic moment was over: now Scott had to convey the news and its meaning to the rest of the world, via the BBC and AP. There was no time for reflection: the deadline was fifteen minutes away, and with a horrible grinding noise coming from the Volkswagen engine we fairly flew back to Monrovia, waving to bemused soldiers at the road-blocks. Scott cursed the Liberian politicians, who always did things with no regard for newspaper or radio deadlines (which demonstrated their amateurism). There were two radios in Monrovia from which Scott could transmit: one at the American Embassy and the other at the headquarters of Médicins Sans Frontières. The diplomatic day was long since over, however, so it had to be MSF. This meant driving through Waterside, the district whose commerce – the tiny commerce of the poor – had revived, with the loitering crowds around a thousand stalls blocking the road. Further delay was caused by the uncompromising nature of the few Monrovian drivers, who rather blocked the way than let someone else through first, thus clearing the way for themselves.

Scott missed his deadline. The world was not, however, to be entirely deprived of the news because Reuters' correspondent had not waited for the press conference after the walkout, but had returned straight to Monrovia to transmit. This had proved the right decision, and Scott was mortified by his own error, caused by inexperience, in having remained. Now AP would have to buy its reports from Reuters, and Scott's boss at AP, at this very moment sitting comfortably in Abidjan with his sundowner, knowing nothing of Scott's heroic effort to file his copy, would be coldly furious. There was only one consolation in the situation: communications with Monrovia were so bad that his boss would be unable to convey his wrath to Scott. And no emotion in the world of news-gathering lasts longer than a few minutes.

We went to drown his sorrows in the Olympic Hotel, next door to El Meson. The Olympic was the second hotel to reopen in Monrovia, and was also run by Lebanese. It was somewhat less comfortable (it did not have El Meson's two hours of air conditioning and running water at night, replacing the latter with a daily bucket), but the beer was cheaper, and the rooms were less than a quarter the price of El Meson's. Scott lived there, as did a small group of photographers, two British and one Swiss, who had come to Monrovia in the hope of dramatic pictures. I soon moved in, partly to save money, and partly to join their fraternity. How many hours were we to spend, sitting in the Olympic's restaurant, overlooking the burnt and looted buildings on the opposite side of the street, drinking beer and discussing the Liberian situation!

Would the National Patriotic Front attack ECOMOG? Was Gaddafi continuing to supply it? Would the United States put pressure on Burkina Faso to stop its support for Taylor? We, who a week earlier would have been hard put to name a single Liberian, had transformed ourselves into pundits, and nowhere else in the world seemed of any importance to us. In the evenings, we questioned each other as to where we had been and what we had done during the day: friendly questions, but with just an edge of professional jealousy, fearing that one of us had concealed something of great newsworthiness.

Many Lebanese gathered in the Olympic at night, to eat, to play cards and to chat: for them, life was returning slowly to normal, and one could watch the bigger traders cruising the empty streets of the city in the latest and most expensive Mercedes. In my youth, I should have despised and excoriated as exploitative their philosophy that any political situation could be turned to profit (indeed, the worse the siutation, the easier to make a fortune, provided only that you were not killed). But now I admired it, and the anti-Levantine feeling in West Africa seemed to me just like the anti-Indian feeling in East Africa, a functional equivalent of anti-Semitism. The Liberians were fixated on politics, the Lebanese on trade; I had no doubts which was the more constructive. And if many of the Lebanese had supported the late Doe, it was because, as traders in a poor and backward country, they were unpopular, and hence vulnerable; they needed political protection, being citizens not of a large and powerful state, but of a small and fragmented one which could afford them no assistance in times of trouble.

In any case, I could easily understand the attractions of Liberia for Lebanese traders. Life there was informal, on a human scale and lived at a pace that was far from frantic: Man was not yet dwarfed by his creations. The lack of efficiency in the bureaucracy was balanced by its universal corruptibility, so that nothing was impossible, whatever the law might say. And since much of the local population was notorious for its lack of commercial acumen, it was possible to do well in business with only moderate talents and a few personal connections.

The Lebanese cared little for appearances, and their clothes looked distinctly the worse for having been worn through another humid West African day. Their all-male company was enlivened from time to time by the presence of a prostitute or two, catering – fairly willingly, it seemed to me – to the needs of the younger among them. It was a tranquil scene, and if not morally instructive at least harmless enough.

It was here that we discussed at length war and peace, dictatorship and democracy, and listened with almost ghoulish satisfaction to stories of suffering and loss. I remember in particular one young man, a Congo in the true sense, who joined us in the Olympic for a beer. His house had been destroyed; he did not know where his wife, his children or his parents were. The very uncertainty of their fate was more tormenting, perhaps, than the certain knowledge they were dead would have been. For if they were still alive, they were behind Taylor's lines, and the stories emerging from there were far from encouraging.

'Take me to your country,' he said. 'I have had enough of this damned Liberia. I will cook for you, I will wash for you, I will even clean your shoes. Anything. I won't ask for money. But I must leave this Liberia.'

His eyes betrayed a depth of suffering that made me blush for my own intermittent querulousness over the minor inconveniences (for a person with money) of life in a destroyed city. Strangely, I did not meet many Liberians whose pain was so unmistakably and overwhelmingly present at every waking moment, so that each word uttered was dragged, sighing, from a slough of despond. I recall only a photographer on one of the Monrovia news-sheets, who fended off the despair one could see in his eyes by working to the highest possible professional standard although, to judge merely by results, there was no point in doing so. He could not develop his photographs properly, and they were further ruined by the inability of his news-sheet to print them to a higher grade of definition than a Rorschach test. But he composed his pictures as if it mattered desperately, as perhaps it did: for he now possessed an unequalled archive of photographs that would one day be a national treasure.

I often asked myself, as I walked the streets of the city and heard the sound of laughter emerging from the ruins, why the suffering which the Liberians had endured, and which only a few weeks before my arrival had moved the world (until something more important came along), was not more immediately evident in their demeanour. I could not envisage myself, once I had endured similar suffering, retaining any *joie de vivre*, or remaining open and polite towards strangers. On the contrary, my faith in life itself would have been destroyed; I should have withdrawn into a state of hermetic misanthropy.

The answer to my question (I decided) was partly noble, partly not. Triumph over adversity is a justifiable cause for pride and self-esteem; survival where circumstances conspire against it is a matter of honour, and lends dignity to even the poorest of the poor. But there was also a less reassuring aspect to the resilience I saw around me: it was sustained, at least in part, by the hope of revenge. As medieval depictions of Hell are generally more vivid than those of Heaven, so is thirst for vengeance a stronger psychical prop than the desire for reconciliation. Hatred explains suffering *ex post facto*, which is better than no explanation at all; and those who were unable to dissolve their suffering in hatred suffered longest. I suspected that if genuine peace ever returned to Liberia, as a result of compromise among the politicians, there would be a sudden access of despair.

On the evening of the walkout of Taylor's delegation from the conference, we – the journalists and photographers – sat in the Olympic with our Heineken (which, as the advertisement so accurately says, reaches parts other beers cannot reach) and discussed Taylor's next step. We moved empty bottles about on the table in a vague, geopolitical way: our brief stay in Liberia had made us experts not only on the country, but on military strategy as well. The general consensus around the table was that, having rendered the national conference completely pointless, Taylor could now afford to wait. To attack the better armed and equipped forces of ECOMOG would be foolish; but the countries who paid for these forces, in desperate financial straits themselves, would sooner or later grow tired of financing the Liberian peace. Then the country would fall into Taylor's lap like an overripe fruit. In the meantime, Taylor could continue profitably to export timber and diamonds from the port of Buchanan.

But then we received a startling piece of news which caused us to begin our speculations anew. We learnt that Taylor's delegation had not really walked out of the conference for good and all: it had declared it would return in a week's time, to receive a reply to some proposals it had made. And in the meantime, it would retain observer status at the conference, enjoying the spectacle of the Lilliputian squabbles of its rivals which, in its absence, could resolve nothing.

I felt cheated. My historic moment had not been historic at all, even after the endurance of so much tedium waiting for it. Rather, it had been a mere scene in an elaborate and continuing charade, a fugitive instant in a shadow play.

7

FIELD MARSHAL BRIGADIER-GENERAL PRINCE Y. JOHNSON

I was told by several people, including Captain Jones of the *Steel Trader*, who knew him well, that it was safest to visit the self-promoted Field Marshal Brigadier-General Prince Y. Johnson in the morning. In the afternoons, having drunk much beer and smoked much cannabis, his behaviour was inclined to be unpredictable and dangerous. He switched from hilarity to murderous rage in an instant, and he acted without inhibition at the prompting of his rage. The weekend before I visited him, I was told he had killed seven people; I met someone whose brother had been killed by him on a night when he shot sixteen others; and I heard about his biggest bag, as it were, thirty-two in a night. He was an insomniac, and prowled the darkness with his AK–47.

Scott had personally witnessed one of his killings. He had been in a car with the Field Marshal, who always drove himself at the head of his convoy because he believed that no one else in his entourage was quick-witted enough to respond to an ambush. The Field Marshal noticed a young man at the side of the road who appeared to be stealing a car. He stopped to question the boy, who was seventeen or eighteen years old. The Field Marshal was furious: he abhorred looting and theft. The boy stammered his confession and excuses, and for a moment Johnson had seemed appeased; but then the boy made the mistake of trying to run for it, and Johnson's fury returned.

'Where my AK?' he demanded imperiously, holding his arm and hand stiffly outstretched to receive it from one of his followers, as a surgeon receives a scalpel from a theatre sister. The rest of his entourage, knowing the denouement, dived for the ditch at the side of the road. Johnson mowed the boy down with gunfire, and then calmly resumed his journey, without arranging for the recovery of the body and never mentioning the incident again.

On the other hand, I heard many people praise Prince Johnson. Some, including my driver, even regarded him as the saviour of Liberia. In ordinary times, perhaps, they would have seen his propensity to kill in a different light, but these were far from ordinary times. His conduct was compared not with some abstract notion of virtue, but with that of the other warlords who operated in Liberia at the same time as he. By their standards, he was something of a paragon. His justice may have been rough but it worked, to an extent at least: he was no more lenient on his own men who looted or stole than on the enemy, and the areas of the city he and his men had once occupied were comparatively well-preserved. There was no destruction there for destruction's sake.

But again, I met someone whose story cast Johnson in such a poor light that it was a measure of Liberia's descent into chaos that a man such as he, Johnson, could have been regarded by anyone as a hero. My informant was Dr Ameche, a Nigerian resident in Liberia for more than twenty years. His hospital, the Island Clinic, was the only hospital that had functioned throughout the civil war and had not closed for a single day. Dr Ameche told me that during the war Johnson, at the head of a posse of men, had appeared at the clinic and announced that henceforth Dr Ameche was to treat only wounded soldiers of Johnson's Independent National Patriotic Front of Liberia. Dr Ameche told him that he was a doctor, and therefore could not possibly accede to Johnson's demand. It was his duty to treat whoever needed his treatment, regardless of political affiliation. This incensed Johnson: he ordered Dr Ameche to the wall, against which he was to be shot. Dr Ameche pointed out, however, that he was a very popular man, who had brought much relief to the suffering, and that if Johnson shot him, it would reflect very badly upon him – so badly, in fact, that he thereby risked assassination himself.

This gave Johnson pause. With Dr Ameche still against the wall, he contacted the American Embassy through his walkie-talkie. He announced to the Embassy that he was going to kill the traitor Ameche, but an Embassy official advised him that, if he knew what was good for him, he would do no such thing. It was then that Johnson decided to reprieve the doctor: indeed, he immediately became very affable, and suggested that they drink a beer together.

Dr Ameche had since met Johnson several times. The Field Marshal was always extremely friendly towards him, greeting him as a long-lost companion. He condescended to forget the time when he was about to have Dr Ameche shot; Dr Ameche was able to perform no such feat of amnesia although, for prudential reasons, he was friendly enough in return. Indeed, he found the change in Johnson's attitude towards him, not reassuring, but rather the reverse. If a man can change so rapidly, proposing to kill a man at one instant and have a beer with him the next, what can either his rage or his friendship mean? At what low value must he hold human life? Dr Ameche had no doubts about the diagnosis:

Johnson was a psycopath of the most dangerous kind, charming, charismatic and brutal.

That Johnson was able so quickly to contact the American Embassy (and his immediate deference to their advice) lent credence to the rumour I had heard that his Independent National Patriotic Front of Liberia was actually an American creation. The Americans, according to the rumour, were alarmed by the prospect of Taylor, supported and armed by Libya, coming to power in Liberia, and had therefore encouraged a split in his ranks. The rumour further asserted that Johnson had mysteriously but conveniently found caches of arms hidden in the bush soon after his split with Taylor. Such arms could have been placed there only by the CIA.

Not a sparrow falls in a country such as Liberia but its death is attributed (especially by intellectuals) to the universal *deus ex machina*, the CIA. Whatever the truth of the matter in this case, quasi-miraculous powers are ascribed to the organization in the minds of many millions of people around the world. My own view is that even where the CIA interferes, the results are usually different from those envisaged or intended, and this for the very obvious reason that people are not billiard balls whose trajectory can be calculated with mathematical precision, but autonomous agents who refuse to play the parts laid down for them by others, often for no other reason than to assert that autonomy.

The Americans were regarded in Liberia as omnipotent, in much the same way as I regarded my parents as omnipotent when I was a child. Why had they not intervened to stop the terrible civil war? A few hundred marines would have sufficed, and indeed two hundred *were* landed – but only to secure the evacuation to safety of Americans and other foreigners. It seemed, therefore, that America cared little for Liberia, although the country was America's offspring, or at least its stepchild. After all, the Liberian flag was but an adaptation of the Stars and Stripes, its first constitution was modelled on that of the United States, and Doe had been the creature of the American government, which had granted his government more military and civilian aid than it had granted all previous Liberian governments combined. The Americans had looked with favour upon, if they did not actually inspire, Doe's coup, not because it brought about the demise of an unpopular government, but because the previous President, Tolbert, had sought a *rapprochement* with the Soviet Union, in the hope no doubt of extracting more financial aid from America (but a coup was cheaper). Articles and pamphlets by Liberians appeared regularly, proving (sometimes simultaneously) that America had never fulfilled its obligations to Liberia, that Liberia had never been a dependency of the United States, that Liberia had never been anything but a dependency of the United States, that America had betrayed Liberia by not intervening, and that the failure of America to intervene was the cause of Liberia's tragedy. The angry tone adopted in these efforts reminded me rather of an adolescent who learns that his parents are neither omnipotent nor infallible yet still demand that he both behave like a responsible adult and be home by ten o'clock at night. It was difficult, apparently, for Liberians to believe they were on their own, and that the world was not so much hostile to them as profoundly indifferent.

Even if Johnson had once enjoyed the backing of the Americans, it was generally agreed that he was a spent force in Liberian politics. He had had his moment of glory when he captured and killed Samuel Doe, but he and his men were now confined to a suburb of the city called Caldwell, named for Elias Boudinot Caldwell, clerk of the Supreme Court in Washington and a founder in 1816 of the American Society for Colonizing Free People of Colour in the United States. The suburb was reached by a track off the main road; at the turning was a poster with a large portrait of the Field Marshal and his deputy, Samuel G. Varney. Below them were the words:

GOD BLESS PRINCE Y. JOHNSON AND SAMUEL G. VARNEY

Even though I still knew comparatively little of them, I wondered whether this poster was the work of a closet satirist.

I drove with Scott and the photographers to Caldwell. We had no appointment with the Field Marshal, but this hardly mattered, since he took the view that there was no such thing as bad publicity. We bounced along the dirt road, past houses which were indicative neither of poverty nor of wealth, but of a luxuriously indolent way of life, where time was not a precious commodity and where a modest competence was easily wrested from the forgiving soil. Children ran naked and carefree in the gardens, pursuing chickens and playing games with the minor artefacts of daily life. My mind was irresistibly thrown back to my own childhood in a greyer climate, and it seemed to me that, all things considered, the life of an African child was far preferable, provided only that the politicians did not cause his parents to be killed.

Though we knew Johnson to be a pathological killer, and despite our precautionary decision to visit him in the morning, we were not really afraid of him: even in his wildest rages, it was unlikely he would so far lose control of himself as to kill several white men, and journalists at that. Even at the height of the war, whites were protected by the power of their complexion. When Taylor's men (I was informed) accidentally killed a white American woman at Monrovia's only Zen temple, they were so terrified of the consequences of what they had done that they decided to eat the evidence. Barring such accidents, which can of course happen anywhere, I felt considerably safer visiting Johnson as a journalist than I did visiting large council housing estates in England as a doctor. Both types of visit, however, had their morbid fascination.

We reached the whitewashed perimeter wall of Johnson's little fiefdom, all that remained to him after his attempt to seize national power. Two guards stood at a gate. On the wall beside it was painted a portrait of the Field Marshal in battle fatigues, his hands clasped above his head in triumph and an automatic slung across his chest, with the words

PRINCE Y. JOHNSON
FIELD MARSHALL I.N.P.L.F.
SUPREME COMMANDER
LIBERIAN REVOLUTION FOR DEMOCRACY

painted in red and black letters below. The two guards, one in the red-striped white helmet of Johnson's military police, a crimson sleeveless T-shirt and camouflage trousers, the other bareheaded, in a white T-shirt with the words SPECIAL COMMANDO emblazoned upon it and plain olive green trousers, both in military boots, desperately wanted their photographs taken. We promised to oblige on our return from seeing *Papé*, 'Father' in the local dialect, as Johnson was known to them. And on our return, they posed with mock ferocity in front of the picture of their leader, the one with a gun looking as if he were about to make a bayonet

93

charge. They took a child-like delight in the repeated clicking of the cameras, not realizing that photographers are distinctly sniffy about posed pictures (unless they arrange the poses themselves) and therefore that many of the 'clicks' corresponded to no movement of the camera shutters.

Back in the Olympic, when we ran short of other things to talk about, we discussed the ethics of photography and the question of whether it was ever permissible, for the sake of art, for photographers to improve upon the arrangement of things (including bodies) as they were found, as it were, in nature. The British photographers argued that it was sometimes permissible, because it was equally possible to lie with the camera by means either of the selection of what was photographed in the first place or of subsequent editing. (How many people realized, for instance, that the famous picture of the Vietnamese girl running screaming along the road originally included a host of press photographers trotting alongside her taking pictures, who were later edited out, Trotsky-like, in the interests of higher historical truth?) But the Swiss photographer, Michel, argued that it was impermissible under any and all circumstances to rearrange things as they were found: indeed, he appeared shocked that his British colleagues should already have slid so far down the slippery slope of amoral relativism. Needless to say, the discussion had some bearing on writing as well as photography, but I remained tactfully silent.

Scott secured our trouble-free entry into Johnson's stronghold by the donation of two cigarettes to the guards, who received them with glee, but were not quite as ecstatic as the two Frelimo soldiers I recalled on the road from Beira to Zimbabwe, who literally danced (barefoot) for joy when I gave them a single cigarette between them. (And when I arrived in Tanzania, I discovered that cigarettes were sold in the market by neither the carton nor the pack, and not even by the whole cigarette, but by the single inhaled drag.) We continued on our way and a mile or two further on arrived at Johnson's house. Surrounding it was an astonishing collection of luxury cars: Mercedes, BMWs and even a Jaguar. There were stranded American monsters, too, in mourning for the expressways they had exchanged for the rough laterite roads of Africa, and tinted-windowed four-wheel drive vehicles of the type favoured by death squads in Latin America. Whatever else one might say against Johnson, his collection of cars made it clear that he was no starry-eyed egalitarian.

Johnson was just emerging from the house with his entourage. He was powerfully built, of average height, and dressed in a chic green jumpsuit. On one breast was pinned a brass scorpion, the badge of his movement; on the other, military decorations, whether self-inflicted I never asked. He wore dark glasses and in his hand, almost like a child's comforter, he carried a sophisticated walkie-talkie. Seeing a delegation of foreigners, he at once began to bark importantly into it. His anxiety to impress with his command of technology was so transparent that it would have been endearing or comical, had one forgotten that only a couple of days beforehand he had killed seven people with a similar command of technology.

He aborted for the moment the tour of his little kingdom that he was about to make, to grant us an audience. Publicity came first. There was no doubting his charisma: in any crowd of men he would have drawn attention to himself, not by his antics but merely by his presence. There was nothing small about either his gestures or his emotions; when he smiled, his broad row of sparkling white teeth reminded me of a shark.

Not that he had no sense of humour: quite the contrary, he was enormously entertaining and possessed of a fine wit. Later, when I saw him speak at Dr Tipoteh's meeting, I admired the consummate ease with which he held the attention of hundreds of people and made them laugh. The timing of his witticisms was impeccable: his performance uplifted the heart and completely disarmed criticism. As Michel put it, if Johnson ever gives up shooting people at night he should be given a television show. It would be an enormous success. So expansive was his personality that I wondered whether, in the absence of an audience, it ceased to exist altogether. Was Johnson ever reflective, contemplative, melancholy, nostalgic? Did he ever stop to think about the people he had killed, or did he live in an eternal present, untrammelled by the past? For all his enormous presence, there was something insubstantial about him.

He took us to an open meeting house nearby, reminiscent in style of an eastern *diwan* in which the vizier of a potentate would receive petitions from the potentate's poor subjects. He sat at one end of the meeting house, and we at the other, he on a high upholstered chair with a coffee table before him, we on plain wooden chairs. He then signalled that we could approach him to take photographs, which we all did. With the cameras clicking and the flashbulbs flashing, he barked more peremptory orders into his walkie-talkie. Whether there was anyone to receive them, I cannot tell: but no reply was audible.

On his left sat a man whom he introduced to us as 'the vice-Field Marshal' – that is to say, Samuel G. Varney, he upon whom the advertising hoarding had called God's blessing.

The vice-Field Marshal was dressed in a stone-coloured safari suit and wore glasses with heavy silvered rims. Behind

1. President Tubman outside the Masonic Hall

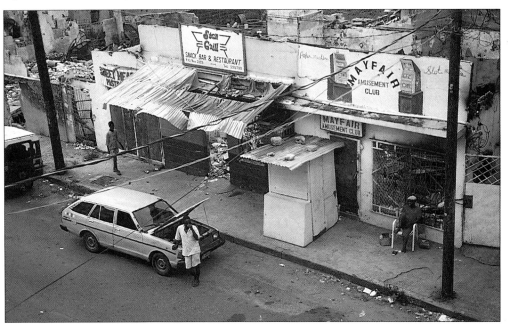

2. The Mayfair Amusement Club and Star Grill in downtown Monrovia

3. The Liberian Institute for
   Biomedical Research

4. Field Marshal Brigadier-General Prince Y. Johnson

5. Inside the Maternity Hospital

6. Outside the Maternity Hospital

7. The Masonic Hall

8. The Harvey S. Firestone Building at the University

9. The University Library

10. Dr Togba-Nah Tipoteh,
    formerly Rudolf Roberts

11. A Masonic Grandmaster gestures to the ruins

12. The beach at West Point, with the Ducor Palace Hotel, seat of the Interim Government, in the distance

13. A street scene

14. Prince Y. Johnson disclaiming ambition

his glasses his eyes seemed hardly to move at all, except in little furtive saurian swivels. His face was expressionless and immobile as a mask; when introduced, he did not smile or in any other way display recognition of the people before him. And his eyes were dead; they did not shine with the light of the soul, but rather spoke of some deep, fathomless emptiness within which only cruelty, suspicion and death could fill. Although it was as hot and humid as ever in the meeting house, a glance at the vice-Field Marshal was sufficient to make one's blood run cold.

Of course, I wondered whether my perception of him was determined by what I already knew of him. In Johnson's entourage we had briefly met a sixteen-year-old who had blood-soaked bandages around both shins; his right arm was in a sling into which blood and serum had also seeped. He told us that he had recently been shot in three limbs by the vice-Field Marshal, who had conceived the insane idea that he was having an affair with his, the vice-Field Marshal's, wife. He was lucky, then, to have got away with his life; but I thought he was still very much in danger. If the vice-Field Marshal were pathologically jealous, it was unlikely his delusion would simply fade away; indeed, it would be sustained by his notorious intake of drugs and alcohol. And the vice-Field Marshal was not a man with scruples when it came to extinguishing life.

I heard from a woman whose husband had gone missing during the war that she had fled for safety (as she imagined it) to Johnson's camp with her own and some neighbours' children. At that time, Taylor's men were rampaging through the district in which she lived, looting and killing indiscriminately. She arrived with the children in the Caldwell stronghold, and was taken to see the Field Marshal and the vice. The latter did not believe she was who she said she was: it was evening, and he had probably been smoking dope and drinking all day. He took a hand grenade from his belt, and made ready to pull out the pin and then throw it into the midst of the little group of refugees. Only Johnson restrained him, itself a rare event, for the vice-Field Marshal was not usually amenable to reason or restraint. The woman owed her life and the lives of her children to Johnson, therefore, though it was his deputy who had threatened them in the first place; and she had incomprehensibly (to my way of thinking) come to the conclusion that Johnson was a good man. The fact that her life had been threatened equally by all the factions in the civil war, and only Johnson had saved her, no doubt affected the way in which she looked at things.

I asked the young man with the shot limbs why he stayed in the Johnson camp at Caldwell. This, of course, was the question of a man who, having been brought up in an ordered society, had never known what it was to live in an arbitrarily dangerous one. True, I had been in dangerous situations; but such was my fundamental faith in the rationality of life that I had never believed the danger really applied to me: I was exempt from it. But the young man who had been shot by the vice-Field Marshal stayed in Caldwell for the simple reason that he would be killed as a traitor to the cause if he tried to leave.

Johnson held forth expansively in his chair, a bodyguard in a blue suit hovering in the garden behind him. The Field Marshal claimed, among other things, that it would be easy for his INPFL 'to flush out' Taylor's men the moment the signal was given, and that only the Liberian people's desire for peace after so much war held back what he called 'the flushing'.

When asked how many men he had under arms, Johnson

replied, without the faintest scruple or hint of embarrassment, 'Sixty thousand'. This, of course, made him a real
field marshal, and not the leader of a mob of a thousand or
fifteen hundred men (according to the best estimates) who
were a disciplined force only by the standards prevailing in
the Liberian civil war. I think that at the moment he uttered
his absurdly inflated figure he actually believed it, and
therefore was not lying. As for the vice-Field Marshal, he
sat imperturbably motionless throughout his leader's performance. Comparing Johnson's flamboyance with Varney's
cold demeanour, I thought I should not care to be the leader
of an organization in which he was my deputy.

The interview, if such it can be called, lasted only a few
minutes. It strengthened my impression of a man who not
only craved, but drew his whole being from, the attention of
others. Without an audience, he was nothing, a puppet with
its strings cut. He repeatedly said that he had no desire to be
president of Liberia, that all he had ever wanted was to rid
the country of Samuel Doe, and that he was ready now to
retire into private life. (His favourite slogan was 'The guns
that liberate should not rule'.) But it was hard to imagine
Johnson pottering about quietly in retirement, gardening or
collecting stamps: and opinions varied as to his true goals.
Some said he wished to go into gilded exile in Miami,
surrounded by beautiful women and with unlimited access
to drugs, while others said his oft-expressed lack of interest
in the presidency was a sham, a ploy to disarm the unwary,
disguising an insensate lust for power. He had sometimes
said he wanted to turn to preaching, no doubt of the
flamboyant and lucrative evangelical kind, and indeed I was
told that at the beginning of his career in the Liberian army
he had spent several years as a military preacher. His
fulminations against sin would be well worth hearing, and I

99

do not think he would have any difficulties at all preaching the commandment against killing, any connection of his words with reality or his own behaviour having been long since severed.

There remained for us the final act of Johnson's performance for foreign visitors to Caldwell: a brief visit to the orphanage he had established there for orphans of the war. The Red Cross had repeatedly asked that the orphans be transferred to their care, but Johnson refused, because he needed the orphanage for propaganda purposes, to convince the world that he was, like all warlords, dictators, terrorists and megalomaniacs, a lover of children.

Johnson climbed into one of his new four-wheel drive vehicles, his mulatto wife beside him, her pale skin a symbol of his power. She had remained silent throughout the interview, like the vice-Field Marshal, but her silence was of a different order: that of the obedient and submissive wife of a big potent chief. Before leaving the house Johnson barked a series of instructions to his subordinates, not so much (I surmised) because he wanted things done, as to impress us with his importance. 'Beat your own people and others will fear you', as the Russian proverb says. On the door of Johnson's vehicle (which, as ever, he drove himself) was a short slogan:

LIBERIA FOR THE LIBERIANS

As with most of his other sentiments, it was difficult to take his xenophobia seriously, and this, at least, was in his favour.

We followed, somewhat limpingly, in our Kombi. The orphanage was only a few hundred yards away, but by the time we reached it a good proportion of the four hundred or so orphans there had been herded on the step outside to meet their benefactor and us (no offer was made to show us around inside). Johnson moved smoothly into photogenic children-loving gear, patting the small children nearest him on the head and explaining that, but for the intervention of his forces, they would all have been dead. He was jovial, and the children laughed and smiled; he turned his attention to one of the smallest of them, and gave a playful smack on his protuberant belly, the sign of malnutrition or heavy worm infestation.

'What the matter with you?' Johnson asked, laughing. 'You pregnant-o?'

His henchmen and sidekicks took their cue and laughed heartily. Some of them probably knew the cause of the child's 'pregnancy' (he was by no means the only orphan in such a condition), but to have corrected the leader's ignorance, or even to have hinted at it by lack of mirth, would have been foolhardy. Just how foolhardy was demonstrated only a few moments later when one of the staff of the orphanage emerged from the building and said to Johnson, 'Chief, the children have no soup for a month.' (*Soup* is the West African term for the savoury accompaniment to the staple starch of the diet.) As one might have expected, Johnson did not react by sympathizing with the poor little mites over the absence of soup from their meals. To the contrary, he exploded wrathfully.

'Why you come now to tell me there no be soup for the children?' he said. 'Can't you see these visitors, foreigners? Why you tell me no soup now?'

The man muttered something about taking the opportunity of Johnson's presence at the orphanage (from which I deduced it was not regular) to ask, but Johnson interrupted him angrily, telling him to address himself to the quartermaster, who was the proper channel for this kind of thing (field marshals don't concern themselves with orphans' soup), as the member of staff should have known very well. The latter had brought some kind of requisition form for Johnson to sign, but he rejected it with a furious toss, and stormed back to his vehicle, the happy little orphanage tableau having been brought conclusively to an end. Another functionary chose the moment Johnson had settled into the driver's seat to present him with a document to sign, with the result that it was soon shredded into confetti and hurled to the ground from the driver's window. Johnson and his still silent, possibly somewhat paler, wife roared off, leaving an angry swirl of dust behind.

I wondered whether the life of the man who had asked for soup for the orphans, and had thus spoiled the Field Marshal's advertisement for himself, was now in danger. I could only hope that the Field Marshal rages were as transient as his affability.

8

THE FIELD MARSHAL AT WORK

It was Captain Jones of the *Steel Trader* who first told me about the video film of the capture and interrogation of President Samuel Doe by Prince Johnson and his men. It sounded gruesome, and I was relieved, on the whole, that Captain Jones had left his copy of the film ashore. It was probably not the best tonic for seasickness. I subsequently learned that there was a black market in the film, and that it was available even in London, for £100. Indeed, with the debilitated state of the Liberian economy, it was perfectly possible that the film was one of the country's most important exports. I resolved to see it.

I mentioned my wish to a Liberian friend and he said 'No problem'. He himself possessed a copy; he knew a friend with a video player, and another with a generator, and if I were prepared to pay the cost of the fuel, a special viewing could easily be arranged. And he would be honoured if I would eat with his family beforehand.

The house was in a suburb of Monrovia, near the Spriggs-Payne airfield (Spriggs-Payne was a nineteenth-century president of Liberia). The soldiers manning the road-blocks in this area were Ghanaians, who had a better reputation than the Nigerians, and certainly were very friendly. Several times when I was in the area they asked me to give a lift back to town to the Liberian girlfriends who had spent the night with them, consoling them for their separation from their families. When I agreed, as I did always, their smiles were more than sufficient reward (no one smiles like that in Europe). The Liberian girls, who wore flimsy dresses, too much bright lipstick and sunglasses speckled with glitter, and had stiffly-lacquered straightened hair, were generally rather dour by contrast, as if they were aware of the accusation levelled at them by some, that they had betrayed the fatherland by sleeping with its occupiers in the hope of laying their hands on the salaries paid in US dollars (insofar as they were paid at all, which was rarely).

To my surprise, my friend's house had a large and by no means ill-kept garden, with frangipani and avocado trees, surrounded by a breeze-block wall. The single-storey house was large too, with a wide verandah at the front. Though the house was not well furnished, its spaciousness and verandah gave it an air of comfort, for space and coolness were more valuable in this climate than possessions, which in any case the climate and termites had a marked tendency to destroy.

I was greeted by my friend's wife, a woman whose skin had the colour and smoothness of dark chocolate. She was slender, with the prominent eyes that a wasting fever sometimes gives. Her attractive face, with hollows sunken at both cheeks and temples, betrayed a quick and acute intelligence; she had a quiet self-assurance that allowed her to meet everyone on genuinely equal terms. She was supervising many children in the garden when I arrived, as finely graded in size as the pipes of an organ, and some of whom must have been her own. I have, however, long since ceased trying to work out how many people there are in an African household, or the complex relationships between them.

Such households must provide an emotional security and support of a kind that I, at any rate, would find stifling.

My friend's wife was not only intelligent, but cultured. Literature was her particular interest. On the shelf where she kept her books I noticed Henry James, Thomas Hardy and even Salman Rushdie, represented by *The Satanic Verses*.

'It is a bad book,' she said. 'Boring and difficult to understand.'

She had seen and experienced too much in the recent war to tolerate gladly the antics of authors who tried to eke out their experience of life with the gimcrack literary tricks of post-modernism. Fantastic verbal contrivances can hardly interest those who have lived with Doe, Taylor and Johnson.

Her life had been endangered several times during the war. First Doe's men came, looking for members of the Gio and Mano tribes (to which she belonged) to kill. They surrounded her garden wall, but fortunately she and her husband kept two large Alsatian dogs, who held the soldiers at bay. (It was a tribute to Liberian military training that two dogs could drive several soldiers off, though they were armed with automatic weapons.) She and her husband fled, knowing that the soldiers would return at night with reinforcements. They did, and this time not only killed the dogs, but cooked and ate them. Then they looted the house of everything.

Taylor's men came next, looking for Krahn and anybody who had achieved honorary Krahn status: that is to say, those who had been employed by Doe's government. She had once worked as a secretary in a ministry, enough to earn a death sentence from Taylor's men, but she managed to conceal from them the fact of her previous employment.

They made her talk in Gio, to prove that she was from Nimba County as she said: failure in such language examinations, conducted by drunken or drug-intoxicated soldiers of fifteen, usually proved fatal. Despite everything that had happened to her (or perhaps because of it) she had attained an impressive serenity: she spoke without bitterness or dramatization, but calmly and not without humour, as if she were relating things that had happened far away and long ago.

She told me the story of a Krahn woman who lived nearby, which was as astonishing as something out of Grimm. When Doe's soldiers were approaching the area, her neighbour, a Gio woman, brought her children to the Krahn neighbour for protection while she herself fled into the bush, knowing that she might never see her children again. The Krahn woman promised to protect them as best she could; and when Doe's men arrived, she claimed the Gio children as her own, thus saving their lives.

A few days later, Taylor's men (or boys) arrived, thirsting for Krahn blood. They found the Krahn woman and were about to cut her throat, when the children whose lives she had so bravely saved, at the risk of her own life, interceded. By speaking Gio to Taylor's soldiers, they persuaded them that the Krahn woman should continue to live, and her life was spared. Thus the story had a happy ending – except that the mother of the children had yet to reappear. Whether she was still alive, no one knew; but in the circumstances, the mere survival of her children was a triumph.

I went inside the house to eat. Eating with the family turned out to be eating in solitary splendour, as guest of honour; a small child, overcome by curiosity as to whether the white man ate by putting food in his mouth, chewing it and swallowing, would from time to time stare at me through a gap in the louvred window or through a door left ajar, before being hauled back out of sight. The food, served in dishes covered by little nets to keep the flies off, was dried fish cooked in cassava greens, a little palm oil and red pepper, and glutinous boiled rice. I found Liberian food monotonous (and always lukewarm), if tasty, but perhaps the aftermath of a civil war is not the best of times to savour a national cuisine. In Liberia, having anything at all to eat was not to be taken for granted.

In addition to the fuel for the generator, I paid for the beer to accompany the performance. The whole family gathered round the video: the generation of electricity alone was something of an occasion in these difficult times, and the addition of beer made it festive. After a few false starts, during which the generator protested volubly, the screen flickered into life, or at least into activity, and the family settled into their seats, or shuffled their buttocks on the floor, in the manner of people about to watch a long-time favourite television programme.

The screen went grey and then a slightly muffled fanfare sounded. Some words rolled down on to the centre of the screen:

THE CAPTURE OF SAMUEL DOE

BY

PRINCE Y. JOHNSON

AND

THE GALLANT MEN AND WOMEN

OF THE I.N.P.L.F.

SUNDAY SEPT. 9, 1990

The video opens with a shot of Johnson. He is in his headquarters, sitting in triumph at a table with a couple of cans of Budweiser on it. Above his head is a picture of a very Aryan Christ. There is an excited hubbub in the room: the camera switches to the floor in front of Johnson's table. There is the cause of the triumph and excitement: the captured President Samuel Doe, sitting on the ground with his arms tied behind his back, his bare legs tied in front of him. He has been shot through both shins.

Both sound and picture quality are poor: there is a constant fuzz on the screen, and all speech sounds as if it has been uttered through a mouthful of hot potatoes. In addition, the English is of the West African variety, and though I have been several times to Nigeria, I am not yet fully attuned to it.

The first words I understand are those of Doe, plaintively directed both at the generality and at the man who holds his fate in his hands:

'Gentlemen, we are all one, Prince.'

It is too late for that kind of sentiment now. The vice-Field Marshal pats Doe on the head, and others follow, first to reassure themselves that the man they captured is really Doe, the man who held the country in his grip for a decade, and then condescendingly. Amidst all the hubbub it is difficult to believe that this frightened and friendless man on the floor was only recently at the pinnacle of power, whose glance caused men to tremble, whose whim was law, whose utterances were the cynosure of a hundred flatterers.

Doe wears a bullet-proof vest, but this is soon ripped off his back. Now he sits naked on the ground, or nearly so: the folds of his fat cover his groin, so that it is impossible to see whether he still wears underpants.

His body is soft, like that of the fat boy at school or, less charitably, like that of a queen termite; his smooth skin glistens with years of good living. Power has not only gone to his head: it has gone to his stomach. When he led the coup, he was almost a starveling; now he looks like a man who eats five meals a day, all saturated in red palm oil. The disconcertingly messianic stare of his early days in power, when he finished his addresses to the nation with the mindlessly demagogic words, 'In the Cause of the People the Struggle Continues!', was soon replaced by a facial expression of adipose complacency. His years in power did not age him, but they changed him, from an incipient zealot to an accomplished glutton.

From time to time, one of the crowd in Johnson's room pours water, or even beer, over Doe's almost perfectly round head, little glistening droplets momentarily shining like *diamanté* in his thick black hair. Whether this liquid is intended as succour or further humiliation it is impossible to tell; but involuntarily, one thinks of the sponge of vinegar offered Christ on the cross. Doe, of course, is not entitled to more sympathy than is any man, defenceless and shot through both legs, surrounded by a host of tormentors; but surely it is a normal human response to feel the deepest compassion for a man situated thus?

No, it is not. The family with whom I watch the film laugh at every indignity heaped upon the late president, though they have watched the film many times before, and greet each one like the punchline of a well-remembered joke – with cries of delight. They are unquestionably normal, these people with whom I watch the film, yet they feel no compassion. On the contrary, they wish only that they could themselves have participated in the torment of Doe.

I make excuses for them: they are good people, my friends for the evening, who have been driven from their normal gentleness to vicarious cruelty by a hard school of experience. But then a still small voice within asks: what torturer does not excuse himself on the grounds of the hardness of his experience? And what if their delight at the rough justice meted out to Doe is delight, not at the justice, but at the roughness?

The camera is held by a Palestinian journalist, who sometimes relinquishes it to someone else and briefly appears, thin and sallow, on the screen himself. He represents an Arab news agency in Liberia, but mystery attaches to his person. People know nothing of his past, and his closeness to Johnson at the moment of his triumph suggests to some, at least, that he is more than just a stringer for an obscure news agency.

It is hot in the room where Doe is held, and the ambient temperature is raised by the presence of so many excited people. The camera switches back to Johnson: he is drinking Budweiser and as he lifts the can to his mouth a young female acolyte steps forward to wipe the sweat from his brow, like a nurse in an operating theatre performing the same task for a surgeon. The surgeon, of course, wishes to keep his germ-bearing sweat out of the patient's wound; but Johnson wishes to impress watchers of the film with his power.

He takes up his walkie-talkie and shouts 'Tango, Tango, Tango, come in Tango!', but does not ask for silence around him. If there is anyone at the receiving end, he must find the message indecipherable. The medium *is* the message, however: Johnson is the only one in the room with such a walkie-talkie.

I can make out only the odd sentence or two in the sound-track, emerging above a chaotic noise that is like the panic that breaks out on an Indian railway platform as a train is about to leave. Johnson says to Doe, 'I fool you and I will kill you', meaning that he captured Doe by a ruse (a

110

double-cross, in effect) and now has Doe completely in his power. He takes another swig of beer and has his brow wiped at the same time, as if the beer goes straight from his mouth to his forehead, through which it seeps as through muslin, and then he makes a statement which demonstrates that alcohol has already reached his stomach: 'I am a humanitarian.'

Even the can of beer is a taunt to Doe, whose presidential days are definitively over. Johnson handles the can of beer to underscore the vast gulf that now separates them: he is relaxed, assured of his power; Doe is trussed up like a chicken on the way to market, obliged to plead for his life.

In these the most unlikely of places and circumstances, I think of lines from Shakespeare, only imperfectly remembered, alas:

> Man, proud man,
> Drest in a little brief authority . . .
> Plays such fantastic tricks before high heaven,
> As make the angels weep.

And how like Richard II is Doe who, having been toppled from the highest power to the lowest debasement, alternately pleads for his life and tries to maintain his human dignity:

> What must the king do now? Must he submit?
> The king shall do it: must he be depos'd?
> The king shall be contented: must he lose
> The name of king? O' God's name, let it go.

As for Johnson, what could better capture his capricious power to grant or to take Doe's life, than Richard III's chilling reply to Buckingham when the latter asks for the dukedom he has been promised:

I am not in the giving vein to-day.

Johnson is not in the giving vein today.

He asks Doe what he thinks of bullets now. This question is ironic, for Doe is known to have believed that ju-ju performed by his witch doctor made him invulnerable to bullets. This explains why the precautions he took when going to meet Johnson in the port authority building were so few and so slack.

'God wants you to be successful,' replies Doe. This is probably a shorthand way of saying 'Your ju-ju was stronger than mine': even at this late stage in his career, Doe cannot be true to his African beliefs, but must disguise them with European words. He is, after all, being recorded for posterity on videotape; he does not want to go down in history as a silly savage who died because of a primitive belief in magic. Did he not hold a university degree in political science? Had not honorary doctorates been conferred upon him? How could such a one believe that casting chicken gizzards in the dust would protect him from bullets? He knows he should not have believed it, and yet he did believe it – and still does, even unto death. Ah, he thinks, if only the witch doctor had performed *proper*, powerful ju-ju, then Johnson would be in his power now, instead of the other way around . . .

Everyone surrounding Doe laughs at the recollection of his capture: he was cowering under a table. But suddenly the atmosphere changes. The people with whom I watch the film are talking loudly, so it is hard for me to follow exactly what is going on in the film, but I hear someone say, 'Tell me where the money is or I'll cut your throat.'

Doe's answer is indistinct, but evidently it isn't satisfactory. 'Why is it he doesn't talk?' someone asks. The money in question, of course, is that which Doe has secreted in foreign bank accounts, rumoured to be tens or even hundreds of millions of dollars.

Then I hear Johnson interject.

'Cut his ears.'

The camera roams round the room, not making sense of the chaos, but rather participating in it. And I hear Johnson's voice rise above the noise. 'Where my AK?'

Within a minute, he repeats his order to cut Doe's ears. He gives this order with beer in his hand, and with no more emotion than a man might express while ordering a taxi.

A man appears with a kitchen knife. He grabs Doe's head and cuts off his right ear with a sawing action. Doe screams. So accustomed am I to violence and sadism on film and television that I have to remind myself that this is different: this is not a cleverly arranged special effect, this is a recording of a man being tortured to death. He will not return afterwards to a home in Beverly Hills with his ear intact.

My friends laugh with joy at the amputation of Doe's ear. They slap their thighs and rock with mirth. Should I protest? Is honest delight at cruelty to be preferred to a feigned decency? While wrestling internally with such moral questions, I raise a bottle of Heineken to my lips: just like Johnson, in fact.

Johnson demands the amputation of Doe's other ear. The ex-president's head is seized again and the remaining ear sliced off. His scream is more strangulated, less vigorous this time: his physical capacity to resist is declining.

What part does the Palestinian journalist, who records it with his camera, play in this? Is he in Johnson's power, does he fear for his life if he protests? Or is it all right – laudable even – to cut off the ears of friends of Israel?

113

Perhaps because I have averted my gaze for a few moments, or perhaps because this is an expurgated version of the film, I do not see what – according to reliable informants – happens next: Doe is made to eat one of his own ears. I am a doctor, and I have seen many terrible things, but I do not think I should have been able to stomach Doe's enforced autophagy.

Someone threatens to circumcise him, and then the scene shifts abruptly to the ground outside Johnson's headquarters, where Doe has been carried. He sits naked with the sun beating down on him. Still trussed, he is in the centre of a huge pool of congealed blood – his own.

'My brother Varney,' he says to the vice-Field Marshal, who seems now to be taking the leading part in his interrogation, 'I'm dying. I'm dying-o.'

This is no more than the self-evident truth, and it has an almost unbearable poignancy. *Varney, my brother*, he says: but what does he expect of Varney? He is appealing to the vice-Field Marshal's awareness that one day he too will have to die, and that in the face of eternal extinction all humanity is one. But Doe himself has learnt the lesson too late: far too much blood has flowed under the bridge. Besides, the vice-Field Marshal is not and never was the man to be moved by such appeals: his mind is fixed on Doe's money, not his life, and in a totally inflectionless voice, conveying only monomaniacal determination, he demands to know where it, the money, is.

Doe replies that he wants to speak, but that he has to be untied first. Varney responds with a sentence which I cannot understand without interpretation:

'Samuel Doe, don't bring that thing to me.'

This means, I am told by the family with whom I am watching the film, 'Don't ask me to untie you.' Why ever

114

not? I ask. After all, Doe has already been shot through both legs, he has lost a lot of blood and his life is visibly ebbing away. Because, they reply, Johnson and his men believe that if Doe is untied, his ju-ju will enable him to escape by disappearing into thin air.

I snort, half-amused, half-contemptuous. To my surprise (though by now I should not be surprised), everyone tells me not to laugh: it is true, they say, that if Doe's hands had been untied, he would have been able to escape, to vanish into thin air, because his ju-ju was very powerful. They tell me this earnestly, and there is no doubt that they believe it; yet one of them is a trained engineer. They believe it because to disbelieve would be to admit their powerlessness *qua* Africans in a world dominated by modern technology.

Varney speaks imperiously.

'Doe, what did you do to the Liberian people's money?'

By the Liberian people's money he means, of course, the money on which he and Johnson want to get their hands. The Liberian people have nothing to do with it.

Doe repeats that he cannot speak while tied up, at which Varney exclaims, 'Oh, you stubborn, eh!' Doe denies that he has any money, beyond $500 in the national bank, and that 'I was in the interest of the people'.

'Please, I'm in pain,' pleads Doe, above further hubbub. In response, someone pours some water over his head and someone else comes forward to wipe his face, but is prevented from doing so by a voice which says crossly, 'He's no longer president, he doesn't need that honour.'

The film ends indecisively, with the arrival of Prince Johnson on the scene. My Liberian friends lean back as the screen goes blank, grunting with satisfaction as after a good and filling meal.

Dr Ameche told me that Doe's body was brought to the

115

Island Clinic for display to the public. (Whether he was given a *coup de grâce*, or just slowly expired from loss of blood, I do not know.) The body lay there for several days, to prove to people that Doe was now beyond the help of ju-ju.

Not the least astonishing thing about the film of his final 'interrogation' was the pride Johnson took in it, and his willingness to show it to any passing foreigner. A Swedish television crew arrived in Monrovia while I was there, who went to interview Johnson. He offered to show them the film himself, in the unexpurgated version. It seemed he was completely unaware of the effect this would have on its viewers (Swedish above all), an effect not to be cancelled out by a few minutes' joviality at an orphanage: on the contrary, the joviality would appear the more sinister, even if he were able to maintain it for the duration of the visit.

Two nights after I had watched the film, I took a stroll in the city. Although there was practically no light, apart from the guttering of a candle or a kerosene lamp here and there, I felt perfectly safe, much safer than in the brightly lit streets of London, say. It appears that in the aftermath of a civil war people are little inclined to violent crime: perhaps they have learnt the hard way that law and order have a virtue independent of all other social virtues. It is not, of course, a lesson that they are likely to heed for very long.

The streets, then, were dark and quiet. The buildings, many of them ruined, loomed vaguely in the darkness, and from them issued the sound of conversation, *sotto voce*. In a couple of places there was the chugging engine noise of a private generator, like a house putting out to sea, and I went to look at the miracle of electric light, which one takes for granted until it is no longer there.

Two of the generators were used to produce tiny coloured

lights which flashed and chased each other ceaselessly in thin tubes around the doors to newly reopened discothèques: a few years ago, such a frivolous use of scarce electricity would have outraged me (there were still no schools open in Monrovia), but I have since come to value frivolity more highly.

A third generator supplied a newly reopened video club – a cinema on a small scale. A knot of people lingered outside it, too poor to enter. In various parts of the city I had noticed the walls of defunct video clubs painted with American cultural icons: Rambo, the Incredible Hulk, Robert Redford and so forth. (The representations were surprisingly accurate.) A tout approached me and stuck to me for a while like a piece of chewing gum to the sole of my shoe.

'Psst!' he said. 'Psst! Psst!'

I asked him what he wanted.

'You want to see a film – a nice film? Not expensive.'

'What kind of film?' I asked.

'A good film, a nice film – the death of the late Doe.'

9

GOOD FRIDAY IN MONROVIA

Liberians, I was told, are a religious people, and Good Friday is the most important day of their religious calendar. Several of the founders of Liberia were clergymen, and they brought with them from North America the then current notions of respectability. There was no talk in those days of cultural relativity.

The streets of Monrovia were deserted on the morning of Good Friday. Even the pavement booksellers were gone, from whom I bought such treasures as *Civics For Liberian Schools*, by A. Doris Banks Henries: 'Every child whose parents are citizens of Liberia is rich. He may not have a large amount of money or property. But he has inherited something more important than money and property... Your heritage is our democratic government.' How rich in irony were those bookstalls! Besides the glossy volumes extolling the lives and works of the last three Presidents, Tubman, Tolbert and Doe, written by sycophants and published at the instigation of the presidents themselves, I found a work which, unintentionally perhaps, summed up the recent history of Liberia: *The Last Chance Diet: A Revolutionary Approach to Weight Loss.*

Michel, the Swiss photographer, and I set out in the morning for the large Baptist church on Broad Street.

Neither of us was religious, but it seemed important to witness the observances of the Liberians. On the way to church, almost the only person we passed was a locally-celebrated Lebanese obstetrician, sitting on the pavement outside his clinic, dressed in his surgical whites and wooden clogs, apparently waiting for custom. He looked bored, and I half-expected him to offer us a delivery at a reduced rate, if only we could find a suitable pregnant woman.

Further on, at an intersection in Ashmun Street, both Michel and I looked down at the ground and noticed dark splashes of dried blood on it. It was curious how we both noticed them at the same moment. They were quite large, two inches long and an inch wide at their widest, and must have come from a serious wound, for there were such splashes every two feet or so upon the pavement, as far as one could follow with one's eyes. The injured person must have passed this way since the last Liberian rains, a few months before, for otherwise the bloodstains would have been washed away (it never rains but it pours in Liberia). Like forensic scientists, we determined the direction in which the wounded person must have come from the shape of the splashes, and decided to follow them to their origin.

The excitement of the chase obscured for the moment its rather sinister import. From time to time the splashes would disappear, as if the fleeing man had temporarily bound up his wound, only to reappear after a break of a few yards, as the urge to flee reasserted itself over the urge to stay the loss of blood. It was gratifying to take up the trail again after such a break: we felt we had been both clever and persistent, not having allowed ourselves to be misled.

We followed the trail of blood as it crossed the road (did the wounded man stop to see whether there was any traffic coming, or did he dash blindly across?) and turned the corner. The streets of central Monrovia, being wide, spacious and entirely on a grid pattern, were unlikely to have provided an escapee with much sanctuary and I imagined our wounded man – whose injuries were not natural, of course – running along the streets, stumbling from pain and weakness, his pursuer gliding in sinister fashion in a car along the kerbside, laughingly waiting to administer the *coup de grâce* but wishing to derive as much enjoyment as possible from his victim's terror. Monrovia was making me lurid.

Eventually, after two or three hundred yards, past the appropriately burned-out and looted Beirut Restaurant, the trail turned off the street into a little passageway to an abandoned building. The splashes of blood continued on some concrete steps down to a basement with a broken iron grille. It was very dark in the basement and it took a time for our eyes to adjust from the bright sunlight outside. The smell was damp and organic: mould mixed with excrement. Gradually, the features of the cellar made themselves visible to us: bare walls stained with black mould, a floor strewn with litter and broken fragments of domestic artefacts. The trail of blood ended here: on a crushed carton of take-away fried chicken, to be precise, from a company called 'Best Chick'.

Had this basement been a torture chamber? It belonged, apparently, to the nearby Swiss *pâtisserie*, long since closed. Perhaps the injury had been merely accidental, the slip of a knife while cutting string, for example; perhaps we had wrongly deduced the direction of the bloodstains, and instead of the injured man fleeing this place, he had been brought here by his enemies or had come for sanctuary. Whatever the truth of the matter, there was something in the atmosphere of that basement that made us shudder and seek the sunlight. We continued on our way to the Providence Baptist Church.

121

We were early for the service: the congregation was only just gathering. The women looked splendid in their vivid dresses and matching hats, many of them in gloves despite the heat. Lemon yellow seems to set off dark skin particularly well. The determination of the womenfolk to look their best had, in the aftermath of the disastrous civil war, an almost heroic quality about it. But the atmosphere in the church was decidedly subdued, not – I suspect – for entirely religious reasons.

The church was large and modern, though traditional in layout and slightly down at heel. Behind the altar was a fresco in which both John the Baptist and Christ Himself were conspicuously depicted as white men, though everyone else in the picture was black. Beside the altar was a Liberian flag on a little stand.

As two white men in the congregation we were, of course, almost as conspicuous as John the Baptist and Jesus were in the fresco. A lay church official approached us and asked whether, since there was time before the service began, we should like to see the old Providence Baptist Church next door. It was one of Monrovia's most historic buildings, he said, the oldest church in Liberia.

He was a little hazy as to whether the battleship-grey building, with its square tower, was actually the original founded in 1822, but he claimed that the Liberian Declaration of Independence had been signed there in 1847. Whether this was true or not I have been unable to discover, even from quite detailed histories of the time; but the little church undoubtedly had about it a mysterious patina of historical significance, and I found this African transplant of North American religious respectability oddly moving. It was precisely because it was so alien to its tropical environment that it was so attractive, so *heroic*, in the way that the

122

well-dressed women of the congregation were heroic.

On one of the walls were portraits of the early pastors of the church, including the mutton-chopped Revd Lott Carey. He was the first black governor of the colony that was to become Liberia, and the co-founder of the Providence Baptist Church, of which he was also the first pastor. Born a slave in 1780 near Richmond, Virginia, he abhorred his condition of servitude and taught himself to read. He became a Baptist and worked his way up the slave hierarchy of his plantation, until he was a storekeeper. He saved enough money to purchase his freedom, and was then ordained minister in the Baptist Church. He was early attracted to the idea of returning to Africa, and said on departure, 'I am an African, I wish to go to a country where I shall be estimated by my merits, not by my complexion; and I feel bound to labour for my suffering race.'

He was a man of parts, a preacher, missionary, amateur doctor, administrator and, in the event, a soldier. Ironically for a man who wished to labour for the redemption of his race, he found himself obliged to undertake military expeditions against those members of it – the original inhabitants of the land – who opposed his presence as a colonist. And he died in a strange way: he was preparing cartridges for use against a native leader, King Bristol, who refused to accept the political authority of the colonists, when a candle was placed too near the gunpowder and the resultant explosion killed eight men and mortally wounded Carey. The *African Repository*, the journal of the American Colonization Society, published a poem *in memoriam*:

> Yes, Afric's sunny skies have gleam'd
> On many a scene sublime;
> But more than hope has ever dream'd

123

Is destin'd for that clime.
The chain shall burst, the slave be free
And millions bless thy memory.

It is customary to deride the efforts of the early colonists, or pioneers as they were known, because they were not cultural relativists (as all right-thinking people are nowadays) but believed themselves to be the bearers of a superior civilization despite their worse-than-shabby treatment at its hands. But who can be so unimaginative as not to be moved by the personal trajectory of a man like Lott Carey, born in slavery, self-educated, with an intense – almost physical – longing to be free, intellectually a trifle confused, perhaps, but still striving for what he considered the good, the true and the beautiful? One must appreciate the colossal personal efforts of such a man, even if he was narrowly circumscribed by the conceptions of his own time.

We returned to the modern church, where the service was about to begin. The pastor was a serious young man, dressed informally in a white shirt rather like a Cuban *guanabira*. He looked as if he had known suffering, for there was pain in his eyes. And when the congregation began to sing, the hymns, which in other contexts seem to me dirge-like and hypocritical, were as stirring as great works of art. 'Were you there when they crucified my Lord?' they sang, and somehow the words took on a special, intensely personal meaning for those who sang them. This service was no formality, as religious services often are: it was a collective catharsis, all the more impressive for its emotional restraint (I had expected something more flamboyant, with hallelujahs, trances and passings out). The hymns were interspersed with readings from the Bible – the Authorized Version, I am glad to relate, not one of the miserably telegraphic modern translations. Many times the words 'Father, forgive them: for they know not what they do' were repeated, and people murmured 'Yes', or nodded their heads sadly in agreement. Again, these words had a special resonance for people who had seen the destruction of their city, their families and their livelihoods. Whenever they were uttered, the emotional temperature in the church rose slightly but perceptibly.

I sat next to a Liberian of about thirty years of age. There was something I didn't like about his face, and throughout the service I struggled to put words to my presentiment about him. His facial muscles seemed to have the consistency of still-unhardened putty, heavy yet malleable. His facial expressions were not the outer signs of his thoughts, but rather followed them at an interval, as after a series of calculations.

'Where are you from?' he whispered during a silence for private meditation on a prayer.

'England,' I replied.

'I was in England,' he said.

'Oh, where?' I asked.

'Hendon Police College,' he replied. 'For three months. I learnt many useful things there.'

'You are a policeman, then?'

'I *was*,' he said, 'during the late Doe's time. I am in retirement now.' He uttered the word retirement with something approaching a leer.

Father, I thought, forgive him: for he knows all too clearly what he does, or what he did, and therefore stands in much greater need of forgiveness than the unconscious persecutors of Christ. We sat on small chairs, not pews, and I was able to edge away from him only an inch or two, a small gesture of distaste which he did not notice.

'Where do you stay? in Monrovia?' he asked. 'We must meet again.'

Reluctantly, I told him: he had at best the look of the blackmailer about him, at worst that of the death-squad or torturer. But I never saw him again.

Michel had grown tired of the service: there were no photographs to be had during it. We slipped outside into the fierce sun, intending to return to the church as the four-hour service drew to a close, and went for a short stroll in the deserted streets. We soon came to the Centennial Hall, around which were three monuments. The first was a kind of cenotaph, in the middle hollow of which two gilded but very stiff and comically sculpted statues, of J. J. Roberts, the first President, and W. V. S. Tubman, faced one another in eternal declamatory silence. The second monument was Tubman's tomb, a large white slab at the rear of the Hall. Originally intended, no doubt, to convey the simplicity of grandeur and the grandeur of simplicity, it now conveyed only neglect, with weeds growing through cracks in the masonry. The third and last monument was in a little overgrown garden: a columnar sculpture of Africans, groaning at the base and bursting forth happily at the top. A plaque explained the allegory: 'The concept of the African Struggle from the depth of servitude and subjugation to the zenith of liberation and freedom. The African Struggle continues. Designed Winston D. Richards Liberia 1978. Nichola Cautadella Sculptor Italy 1979.'

In the background there was a metallic flapping sound. It was the wind playing in the abandoned headquarters of the True Whig Party, a multi-storey building in the modernist style of the 1960s, whose metal outer fitments such as balconies had been ripped from the central core of the edifice and left dangling in silvery tatters. Now they jangled

126

in the breeze as bells tinkle in a Buddhist monastery, the only sound in the general silence.

We entered the Centennial Hall. It was a plain rectangular auditorium, not unlike those used for school assemblies. The floor was flat, without a slope to assist those sitting at the back to see. Around the upper part of the wall ran a narrow balcony, from which still hung red, white and blue bunting. The Centennial Hall was where Liberian presidents were inaugurated, and not long before Amos Sawyer, the Interim President, had been sworn in there. The flowers from the day of the ceremony, now dried, brown and shrivelled, remained in rusting metal vases, while hastily written cards, indicating where the Diplomatic Corps and the Armed Forces of Liberia should sit, were stuck to the walls with yellowing sellotape. In the passageway around the auditorium were wooden and plaster busts of famous Liberians (all politicians), some of them toppled from their plinths or with chips hacked from their faces. There was a pronounced smell in the building: people, it seemed, had come to relieve themselves on a certain tradition.

There was a stage and a large area behind it, partly hidden from view by wine-coloured curtains. There, besides the source of the smell, we found three carved wooden thrones with high backs and dark crimson velvet upholstery. They were all toppled over, not carelessly, I thought, and not as the result of a scuffle or a riot, but with almost theatrical precision, as the standards of defeated armies are lowered after surrender. One of the thrones had no lettering, but the two others had *President of the Senate* and *President of Liberia* inscribed in gold on their backrests. The President of Liberia's throne had a higher backrest than the others.

The sight of toppled thrones amid the little piles of faeces dotting the floor was very disturbing. It seemed to signify

127

the complete breakdown of any proper system of authority, without which life is soon reduced to its Hobbesian solitude, poverty, nastiness, brutishness and brevity. Michel and I beheld the scene in silence: and then, at precisely the same moment, we had the same idea. He would take black-and-white still lifes of the destruction of the city, while I would write an article explaining the significance of the destruction. We were both convinced that such pictures – of burnt-out cars, toppled thrones, ransacked libraries, smashed medical equipment – would have a poetic impact stronger than the more obvious subjects. Editors, alas, were not to agree with us.

The presidential throne had a large eye, the white of which stood out very startlingly, carved on the backrest above the velvet upholstery. It was a Masonic symbol. Since the throne was quite new, made in Doe's time, the Masonic eye was evidence that the once hated fraternity had not only survived its persecution but had made something of a comeback. Doe, it was said, had entered the brotherhood, having long proscribed it. Indeed, one of the curious things about the supposedly revolutionary regime of which he was the leader, whose principal justification was the liberation of the native people of Liberia from the sesquicentennial domination of the Americo-Liberians, was its inability to replace the symbols of the old regime with any of its own. Thus, the national motto remained *The Love of Liberty Brought Us Here*, though, of course, the native Liberians had never been anywhere else. The flag of the republic, so obviously American in inspiration, was not changed for one of indigenous design; institutions named after the last two presidents of the *ancien régime* were not renamed; the streets of Monrovia continued to be called after the 'pioneers', that is to say the early Americo-Liberians; and when Doe decided to print the first Liberian banknote, he could think of no one else to portray on it but J. J. Roberts, the first Americo-Liberian President. This failure to produce alternative national symbols was not the result of a mere lack of imagination: it was an accurate reflection of the undeniable fact that the Americo-Liberians *did* found the Liberian state, and that insofar as it had any unity at all, this was owed entirely to the Americo-Liberians. No man can be President of Liberia, therefore, and repudiate utterly the heritage of the Americo-Liberians, whatever his rhetoric or the basis for his political support might be. Since the Americo-Liberian domination of Liberian affairs is a thing definitively of the past (rumours of their support for Charles Taylor notwithstanding), Liberians will almost certainly continue to experience problems with their cultural identity: they will think national but feel tribal, a divorce of thought and feeling that is the perfect nutritive medium for demagogues and charlatans, who lead their followers merrily to destruction.

While Michel took his pictures of the fallen thrones, I explored further the rear of the stage of the Centennial Hall. I came across something that took me aback more powerfully than almost anything I had yet seen. Lying on the ground, casually as it were, was a Steinway grand piano (the only one in the country, as I correctly guessed), its legs sawn off. The body of the piano, still gleaming black and in perfect condition, was in direct contact with the floor, while the three sawn legs were strewn about. Speechless for a while, I recovered and called Michel over: he too was struck dumb.

This was not mere vandalism, in the commonly accepted sense. I imagined how, if I were a vandal, I should go about my business with a piano: I should lay into it (perhaps impotently, for pianos are tough) with a heavy instrument, a

129

mallet for example, and I should go for the keyboard and the mechanism with as much force as I could muster: never for an instant should I think of calmly sawing off the legs. But here the legs were, sawn off with the precision and neatness of a surgeon amputating the hand of a thief in a land of Islamic punishments: he had done his work well, the carpenter of destruction, with skill and devotion. How satisfying it had been to him, how fulfilled he must have felt afterwards! I nearly wept.

Michel and I stood a while like mourners at an interment, and then, recovering the power of speech, we speculated as to whether the amputation of the piano's legs could mean anything other than it appeared to mean: a long-contemplated but long-frustrated revenge upon a whole alien civilization. Perhaps the man with the saw was in search of firewood rather than revenge. After all, the people of Monrovia were using wood from the very fabric of buildings to light their fires for cooking so why not piano legs? There were, however, more convenient sources of wood to hand: even the thrones would have been easier to dismember.

It occurred to me, having witnessed the exportation of heavy construction equipment from the port of Monrovia at a time when such equipment was never more needed and never harder to replace, that an enterprising Lebanese businessman might have set eyes upon the piano, recognized its value, and found a customer abroad for it. Perhaps he sent his men to carry it away but they, finding it would not go through the door, were obliged to saw off its legs for ease of removal. They had no sooner finished their sawing than they were surprised in their work, like ancient Egyptian tomb-robbers, and forced to flee.

But these alternative explanations did not satisfy us: we

returned to our theory of simmering rage and envy that boiled over when civil war removed the restraining lid. Michel took pictures of the stricken instrument, the red, white and blue bunting in the background, while I was content to gaze at it for minutes on end. How long, I thought, before some post-modernist composer has a pianist not play the instrument but, in front of the audience, saw off its legs, to the craven applause of critics afraid to be thought stupid or reactionary?

It was almost with reluctance that we left the Centennial Hall, worried that we had not squeezed the last drop of meaning from the sights it contained. We were saddened by what we had seen, yes, but exhilarated by it too: we felt we had secured something of a scoop. Besides, melancholy is not entirely an unpleasant sensation; it reassures those who experience it that they are of delicate but superior sensibility.

Out in the bright sun once more, which seemed to suck moisture from the paving stones themselves, we were joined by a short man in a light safari suit with a book tucked tightly under his arm.

'Stubblefield's the name,' he declared, like a character out of Dickens, and shook our hands.

He began at once to talk of politics, of the dire situation the country faced, and of the good old days. But which *were* the good old days, that was the question. (Tell me the days a man considers good, and I will tell you what he is.) Well, the golden age, as far as Stubblefield was concerned, was the presidency of William R. Tolbert, Jr.

'I will tell you quite frankly,' he said, 'that Tolbert was not a bad President. No. He presided over an era of unprecedented growth in Liberia. Everything you see around you – roads, buildings, schools – was built by Tolbert.'

131

He swept his hand magisterially around the ruined town-scape. A gust of wind caught the strips of metal dangling from the gutted headquarters of the True Whig Party and gave them a shake, producing a clanging noise like a thunderclap in an amateur theatrical. Taken as a whole, the scene – including burnt-out cars, potholes in the road, uncollected rubbish and eviscerated houses – was not a good advertisement for the solidity of past achievements.

'Tolbert's problem', said Stubblefield, 'was that he was too ambitious and energetic. He was impatient, he wanted to transform the country within a few years, to make it great. He wanted us to *work*.'

Ever since Stubblefield told us his name, it had nagged at the back of my mind. It was not completely unfamiliar to me, and suddenly I remembered where I had come across it before: on a memorial plaque inside the Masonic Temple. So the Stubblefield family (assuming there to be only one of that unusual name) was a member of the charmed circle of Americo-Liberian families which had once so dominated the country. It was scarcely to be wondered at, therefore, that Stubblefield lamented the passing of Tolbert and his government. Doe's coup had made him almost an exile in his own country. And his Americo-Liberian descent explained why, when asked where he was from, he replied stolidly, 'I am a Liberian'. Pressed as to which part of Liberia he came from, he repeated, 'I'm a Liberian, that's all'. Until recently, the word 'Liberian' signified Americo-Liberian to all the tribal people of the country, who called themselves Kru or Krahn or Vai, but never Liberian.

I asked him whether I might look at the volume he carried under his arm. It was leather-bound and gold-tooled, strikingly handsome and out of place in these surroundings. He gladly let me look at it: the *Liberian Law Reports for 1966*.

The quality of the paper alone and of the printing (done in the United States) were sufficient to indicate that, though only twenty-five years old, the book was from a different aeon. It opened in my hand at a page on which a judge delivered his findings in a civil action brought by a plaintiff called Hitler Coleman. Poor Hitler (Coleman, not Adolf)! Could anyone with such a name receive a fair hearing? I glanced through the argument, abstruse and full of jargon. I wondered whether such learned discourse was really a camouflage for the acceptance of bribes, just as elections in Liberia were a camouflage for the maintenance of the incumbent in power; if so, the provision of a plausible legal justification, complete with precedents and jurisprudence, for a decision determined by quite other considerations, was indeed a sophisticated intellectual discipline, worthy almost of admiration.

Stubblefield was a lawyer, one of many among the Americo-Liberians. Presumably, there was not much call for lawyers these days, there being no courts of law, only decrees issued by the President of the Interim Government of National Unity (whom the rebels contemptuously called the Mayor of Monrovia), as interpreted and enforced by the soldiers of ECOMOG. Stubblefield, stout defender of Tolbert and his works, went sadly on his way, his *Liberian Law Reports for 1966* to him what pornography is to the sexually frustrated.

We returned to the Providence Baptist Church for the end of the service. The emotional temperature had not risen. The pastor was concluding his sermon: he asked whether forgiveness should be extended even to the rebels who were now preparing to attack the city. There was gentle laughter in the congregation at the pastor's question: at least on Good Friday, the answer was obvious. Yes, they should be forgiven, continued the pastor, even though they were under demonic influence, for in the last instance, on Judgement Day, we all stood in need of Divine mercy.

The service ended when a visiting pastor from another church, who was dressed in a well-cut blue suit, stood to face the congregation.

'Lord,' he said, 'forgive us our wicked acts.'

The emotional impact of these words on me was somewhat reduced when, a few minutes later, I saw the man who had uttered them drive away with his family in a new and expensive car. He was obviously on his way to a good lunch, to which he had been looking forward for some time. Did this in itself prove that his contrition was insincere? Should we demand loss of appetite among the penitent? If Charles Taylor were to fall into the hands of those who had just agreed to forgive the rebels, how would he be treated? Would his captors say that Divine mercy was one thing, human justice quite another?

We returned to the Olympic Hotel, greatly in need of a beer. There we found the two young British photographers, who themselves had just returned from photographing some aspect of the ruins of Monrovia. I described to them – evidently with some feeling – the destruction of the piano in the Centennial Hall. They looked at me amazed: not that the piano should have been so wantonly destroyed, but that I should consider its destruction as in any way significant.

'It's only a piano,' one of them said, 'an inanimate object.'

I recalled that a book had been written about the attitude of the Chinese Communists to the piano. There was a very close connection between periods of repressive savagery and periods of denunciation of the 'bourgeois' instrument. Later, when I described what I had found in the Centennial Hall to an intelligent and educated Americo-Liberian in exile, he grasped its significance at once. 'It's the rejection of a whole

134

civilization,' he said. 'But the tragedy is that the piano is not just something for the white man to appreciate, though he invented it. The piano is something for the whole of the human race.' But the British photographers insisted that their indifference to the destruction of the piano was in the name of a higher morality.

'What do we care about a fucking piano?' one of them said. 'Thousands of people have been killed in Liberia.'

I despaired then of my own country. How had we come to breed such a race of barbarians?

10

THE KILLING FIELDS

The road from the city towards Spriggs-Payne airfield had evidently been the scene of heavy fighting. The garages, workshops, showrooms and fast-food restaurants at the side of the road were pockmarked by bullets; some had been shuttered with iron grilles as their owners fled (intending, no doubt, to return when peace was restored), while most of the plate-glass windows were smashed by looters and vandals – I recalled Bakunin's stunningly insightless remark that 'the urge to destroy is also the creative urge'. The garage forecourts were littered with wrecked and burnt-out cars, rusting on their haunches and picked over for anything useful which might have escaped annihilation. Everywhere was deserted.

I drove along the road to the John F. Kennedy Hospital in a taxi which progressed by a succession of violent jerks, any one of which might have produced the vehicle's final disintegration, rather than by a smoothly indivisible motion. Nevertheless, it reached its destination: if they avoid outright destruction, cars in Africa – like people – display a commendable resilience.

The hospital was a gift from the United States to Liberia in the early sixties, when it still seemed possible to do unequivocal good in Africa by the simple transference of western techniques and institutions. While Britain dressed up the Speaker of the Ugandan Parliament in a wig and paraded a mace before him, America built a hospital in Monrovia. The wig and the mace were abandoned rather earlier than the hospital, but – from the historical point of view – not very much earlier.

The JFK, as it soon became known, was built to the highest possible standard, scarcely differing in its equipment from a hospital in the United States. The argument for implanting such an institution in the midst of a country which until then had known nothing like it – that Africans should be entitled to the same kind of medical care as Europeans or North Americans – was undoubtedly well-meaning and even noble, though in practice unrealistic. It was expected that a hospital like the JFK would not only fulfil its medical function, but would perform a profound psychological service to the nation and even to the entire African race. The very technical excellence of the hospital, run and staffed by Liberians, would speed recovery from the profound sense of inferiority which centuries of helotry vis-à-vis the white man had provoked in the black man.

Things worked out rather differently, of course. The intellectual fashion changed, and western high-technology medicine came within a few years to be regarded (largely by western intellectuals and public health experts) not as a boon but as a curse for poor African countries such as Liberia. It was argued that the excess mortality in Africa was caused by a comparatively small number of infectious diseases, either treatable or preventable, or both, and it ought therefore to have been possible to train a large number of health workers to tackle these few diseases throughout the land. Central teaching hospitals such as the JFK devoured more than half the health budget of the entire country, serving only the urban population and leaving much of the country without health services of any description. Far from restoring the cultural confidence of the Africans, hospitals such as the JFK merely reinforced their intellectual, technical, economic and emotional dependence. Furthermore, alien institutions like the JFK were bound to fail, even according to their own lights.

And fail it eventually did. At first, though, it functioned properly, achieving high standards, so that for a few years it was one of the best hospitals in West Africa. But it was never quite good enough for President Tubman, who went regularly to Switzerland for his treatment, and died in a London hospital where he had gone at the age of seventy-five for a cataract operation. (It was rumoured that Tolbert had him poisoned there.) No doubt the hospital was never entirely free of corruption, but it *did* treat and cure patients.

That was to change with the accession to power of Samuel Doe. As one Americo-Liberian put it (though he may not have been a wholly unbiased informant), 'Before Doe they were doing open-heart surgery; after Doe you couldn't find an aspirin there.'

The initials JFK took on a new meaning in Doe's time: Just For Killing. It was said that people went there only to die; the maternal mortality rate in the JFK, for example, was more than a hundred times greater than in a European hospital, and it was said that many of the patients caught malaria and typhoid only *after* admission. The hospital's infrastructure deteriorated rapidly: a visiting team of foreign doctors was horrified to discover that not a single lavatory or water tap was working throughout the hospital's four floors. At the same time, the medical director (a Fellow of the Royal College of Surgeons) awarded himself a $62,000 'loan' out of hospital funds to buy himself one of the larger

139

models in the Mercedes range. Nurses refused to attend their patients, unless bribed to do so. Even the mortuary ceased to function, despite the omnipresence of death: the refrigeration system broke down, never to be repaired, and a notice was put up stating that no more bodies could be accepted until the ones already decomposing there were taken away by their relatives.

The hospital was not elegant, even before mortar or rocket fire tore a few holes in its fabric. More than a quarter of a mile long, it was painted an unpleasantly diarrhoeal brown, a colour which is unaccountably popular with administrators of such institutions the world over. There were no windows visible; they were hidden behind fixed concrete louvres, presumably intended to shield the interior from the rays of the sun. The overall impression was of something brooding and sinister, a headquarters for the secret police, perhaps, or an institute devoted to research on the refinement of torture. It was set at some distance from the road, as if to preserve it from prying eyes. It was now guarded by a Ghanaian soldier, lying asleep on a table under a nearby shelter. I woke him and asked whether I might look round the hospital, for I was a doctor. He made no objection: nearly everything that could have been looted had been looted. I thanked him and continued on my way.

Apart from some outlying buildings, which were used as an orphanage run by Médecins Sans Frontières, the hospital was now completely deserted. Several miles of corridor echoed to no footfall but my own; part of the ground floor, dark as night and dank as a jungle, was flooded. There were the kitchens, laboratories, canteen and mortuary. Nothing remained of the kitchen equipment except a few irremovable stainless-steel fitments, while the mortuary's storage refrigerators stood with their doors open, as if in anticipation of a resumption of normal service. A cream-painted metal trolley with an ancient bloodstain had survived the general destruction. The nearby pathology laboratories had been denuded of their instruments and chemicals, leaving only the benches stained with the residues of past investigations. The staff canteen, too, was empty of furniture, only the glass division above the serving counter remaining intact.

More daylight got through to the upper floors. The wards were several hundred yards long, divided into white-tiled, four-bedded cubicles. Without human presence, they were sinister in their impersonality, and it was not difficult to imagine why people from the villages, who lived pre-eminently social lives, and who were rarely out of the sight of their family, friends and neighbours, should have been greatly intimidated by the hospital. In some of the cubicles the bedsteads were still present, with mattresses in various stages of decomposition. Above the beds were outlets for oxygen, though of course no gas had passed through them for many years. The form of a western hospital was there, so to speak, but not its content.

Between the wards were offices and classrooms. In one of the latter I found some dummies resting on beds, which had obviously been used to teach techniques of resuscitation to students. The dummies were of whites of indeterminate sex, and one of the faces had been slightly charred by the application of a naked flame. Although I thought at first that this was a feeble or hastily executed effort at revenge by Liberian insurgents upon the whole of the white race, I swiftly concluded otherwise: the charring was an attempt to make the dummy more lifelike, with a closer resemblance to the patients the students would actually treat.

The offices were either denuded entirely of their contents,

·or in such a state of chaos that they looked as if their looters had been forced to flee in panic in the midst of their activities. The professor of surgery's, for example, had books and papers strewn about in violent fashion: to see books trodden upon, having been hurled at the wall, their pages torn and their spines broken, is scarcely more reassuring than to witness a bonfire of books. Later, I asked in several places what had become of the professor of surgery, a Ghanaian. Nobody knew.

In the office of one of the administrators, I found a table piled with letters, a few opened, most still in their envelopes. One of the former was addressed to the Administrator of the Tubman National Institute of Medical Arts and dated 8 February 1990:

Dear Madam:

We the students . . . from Nimba County who were affected by the fighting in the County are kindly asking you for an assistance as to enable us to complete the academic year 1990 successfully.

Madam Administrator we are financially ill and can not afford to pay the tuition in full this year due to the situation experienced in our county this year. Madam, please allow each of us to pay $130.00 after the mid-year break as total tuition and other fees for the 1990 school year.

In view of your usual assistance and cooperation towards students, and as Administrator, we deem it necessary to acquaint you with our problems and ask for your motherly consideration.

NOTE: Each of us had some terrible experiences up in Nimba and on our way back to Monrovia which have caused us to be in the present state. We would be glad to acquaint you with these experiences.

I opened a couple of the still-sealed letters on the desk: they were now surely beyond any hope of finding their addressee, who had, as far as I could tell, nothing to do with the hospital. They were from schoolboys requesting help from a man called Bob Charles, almost certainly an American missionary: '. . . I'm always trouble for the balance tuition which is about $11.50. The school authority once to send me home for their tuition which is that amount, and I don't want to be disturb by any one of them. As you received this note please try to that day by paying the mission house down there . . .' The second was rather better written but more plaintive still:

Dear Bob Charles;
    I received your letter send to me sometimes ago, and I read it with knowledge and understanding. I would like to say this to you that it is a very hot competition between our friend who always likes to take first place every making period. And myself 2nd. His average was 94% and mine was 93% and because of this he came first again and I came second out of 50 students.
    I'm trying to get in that post with him that's while I have tripple my studies these days. Our pastor told me that he saw you sometimes ago and extended your greetings to me in words which of course is very present-able . . .
    Bob Charles, I'm always embarass among my friends, because I do not have any clothes this year. I'm always in my uniform after school and most especially in social gathering. This has been the cause of one of my uniform trousers being destroyed.

143

In this respect, I am kindly asking to make it possible to buy yards of clothes and be *sew* into some trousers for me. This request is very important to me at this stage. When I'm among my friends I cry with sorrow in my heart and sometimes with tears in my eyes when I'm alone.

Please tried. If only you can do this for me that is to provide me with clothes your reward will be in from God who knows what we do. This is my problem please slove it for me.

These letters were dated 19 October 1982 and 26 June 1983 respectively. Their accounts of suffering – so real at the time, so trivial by comparison with what was to come – had lain unread for eight and nine years, epistles from half an epoch ago.

The paediatric ward was decorated with a mural, depicting a chicken, an elephant, a giraffe and a (white) clown, all somewhat implausibly in a rowing boat. The chicken was larger than the elephant, and looked more like a vast raptor than the familiar domestic bird that pecks the dust in every Liberian yard. Far from reassuring any child, this failed attempt at pictorial jocularity would serve only to terrify him or her further: even I found the roc-like chicken disturbing to look at for very long.

Perhaps the most melancholy sight of all in the JFK, however, was that of the operating theatres on the top floor of the building. It was evident still that they had once been equipped to the highest standard, with everything imported from America, but they were now as unlikely to resume their intended function as Ankor Wat. Instruments rusted in glass and stainless-steel cupboards, operating lamps with smashed bulbs pointed drunkenly at the walls and the ceiling, while operating tables (their state of preservation a

144

tribute to their manufacturers) still serenely awaited their patients.

I left the JFK Hospital through a different door from the one by which I had entered, this time near the maternity wing of the hospital. Volkswagen ambulances lay stricken in the ground; even an official-looking black Mercedes was abandoned as beyond repair. The maternity wing, I was told, had been refurbished by the Japanese only a few years before the civil war (after being allowed to fall into disrepair in the 'normal' way), and now it was the worst damaged part of the hospital. Every time I heard a Liberian say that the country needed aid, that it could not recover without it, and that it was the duty of more fortunately placed countries of the world to provide it, I found myself asking, 'Precisely how many times must a hospital be rebuilt before it functions both properly and continuously?'

However sceptical one may be of the good wrought by western hospitals in Africa (and surely they are by now an inevitable part of African life, for good or ill), the sight of despoliation such as that at the JFK remains very disturbing. For I repeat, the destruction of the hospital was not the result of physical damage inflicted directly by the civil war; still less was it the work of people who had carefully come to the conclusion that hospitals, which absorbed half the national health budget, were a menace to the welfare of the general population: rather, it was an inchoate cry of rage and despair, deep and primitive, such as the disaffected youth of large conurbations in Europe and America utter when they disfigure public property or resort to drugs.

Leaving the hospital to the further depredations of time and climate, I returned in the direction of the city. There were several sights along the way I wished to see. The Ahmed Sékou Touré National Archives Building overlooked the road: it was closed, of course, its plate-glass door punctured with neat bullet holes. The building, as far as I could tell, was now empty of papers; they had either been looted, burned, or moved away for safety. It was possible that the nation's entire historical record had been destroyed or irredeemably dispersed. No doubt the British photographers would have thought this a matter of no account – 'Who cares about a lot of old papers when so many people have died?' – but even Samuel Doe, in whose first term of office the archives were built, appreciated the importance of preserving the records of the past. Laying the cornerstone of the new building in 1982, he said: 'As we have set out to improve education in our nation, we consider it imperative to reflect upon the past, through our literature and art . . . We hope this Center will serve as a source of great enlightenment for generations of Liberians.'

The following year, he rather spoilt the impression by opening the archives in the presence of Sékou Touré of Guinea, after whom the building was named in recognition (as Doe said) of his 'many outstanding contributions as a great African intellectual, scholar and good friend of Liberia'.

To call Sékou Touré a great intellectual and scholar is rather like calling Genghis Khan a great architect, for he ruined his country no less comprehensively than invading Mongols would have done. He killed or forced into exile a third of its population, destroyed its infrastructure, relentlessly drove down the general standard of living and introduced a reign of terror as absolute as any in the world. Better a million illiterates than one intellectual like Sékou Touré.

Not far from the ex-archives is St Peter's Lutheran Church. It is a modern building, nondescript in the way of present-day suburban churches (unlike the new Anglican Cathedral of Monrovia, a brutally angular building of stark concrete through which a black and mouldy stain inexorably seeps). Outside St Peter's a notice still stands:

COME AND LET US GLORIFY GOD TOGETHER

Next to the church is a school building. Both were deserted when I arrived. In the small garden in front of the church there are two slight mounds, long and narrow. These are the mass graves for about half of the six hundred people who took refuge in St Peter's and were massacred there at the end of July 1990.

I entered the church, which was open. There were no pews or chairs, just empty floor space. The altar was a large, bare table. On one of the walls the numbers of the hymns were still posted: 532 and 191. The concrete floor was covered with a blackish substance, dry and in some places powdery. I looked a little closer: it had a reddish or maroon hue. It was blood.

Towards the walls one could make out silhouettes in the dried blood, silhouettes of bodies in contact with the ground where the blood had consequently been unable to run. I was seeing it nine or ten months after the killing, and no one had yet cleaned the floor. Perhaps it was being preserved as a national monument, but I doubted it.

The people killed were all Gio and Mano, from Nimba County. During the civil war they had gone for sanctuary to St Peter's, fleeing the tribal fighting in the city, no doubt imagining that all sides would respect the sanctity of a church. But one day the Armed Forces of Liberia, maddened by the imminent prospect of annihilation, arrived and shot them all. It was said that Doe himself had participated

147

in the massacre, arriving in a large white car (presumably a Mercedes). This was no more than a rumour, of course, and was unprovable; such was the chaos reigning at the time that the bodies went undiscovered for three months, until after Doe's capture and death. Even the responsibility of the Armed Forces of Liberia was an assumption based on past behaviour: a fair enough assumption, therefore.

I walked into the school. On the wall of the entrance hall was pinned one of those cards printed with a pious sentiment which one sometimes finds in the suburban homes of the conventionally religious:

I will die, but that is ALL I will do for death.

In one of the rooms I found a small black book, printed on fine thin paper in the United States. It was a New Testament with the Psalms appended, a gift of an American religious charity devoted to spreading God's Word in heathen parts. Inside the front cover were the printed words *Presented to:*, with a name filled in by hand: Martha D. Z. Sonyah, 20.7.90. Inside the back cover were the printed words *My decision to Receive Christ as My Savior*: and a date filled in by hand: 21.7.90. One day elapsed, then, between her receipt of the book (probably given her on the day of her arrival at the church) and her achievement of religious conviction: as the pastor of the Providence Baptist Church told me, in difficult times people turn more easily to God.

Eight days after she was given the book, and seven days after she invited Christ to enter her heart (as I believe the evangelicals put it), Martha D. Z. Sonyah was killed, along with six hundred others.

I held the frail black book open in my hand, almost as a

small bird with a broken wing. I examined the childish writing and imagined Martha, sixteen years old perhaps, pretty with her hair done into the elaborate patterns into which African girls often comb their hair, smiling gaily and approaching life as if it were a trifling affair of no great consequence. Even her necessary flight to sanctuary in St Peter's had not extinguished her *joie de vivre*, even now she laughed and was unafraid, for the difficult times would surely soon be over. Her conversion, if that is what it was, signalled no great change in her life, since she had always been religious in an unthinking way: she filled in the date of her deliverance from sin as much to oblige others as to assure herself of eternal life (which she regarded as eternal anyway, as we all do until much later in our lives).

I imagined the powerful white car (with darkened windows) in which Doe travelled, drawing up silently outside the church. I imagined the soldiers bursting in, shouting and firing indscriminately; I imagined the bodies, Martha's among them, falling on top of one another. Screams, writhing, silence.

I closed the book gently and put it back where I had found it. I am not emotional, but my hand was trembling.

Scarcely more than two hundred yards from the church was Mrs Doe's house. It, too, was painted brown in the manner of an institution for undesirables or incurables, and it was surrounded by a high wall of the same colour. Mrs Doe had evidently not been a nature lover, to judge from the yard of her house, which was all concrete and no garden. There was, however, plenty of parking space which, in her heyday, was probably very necessary. Perhaps Liberians are too closely acquainted with nature as children to be sentimental about it as adults: what they admire are electric kettles and portable telephones.

149

At the time of her husband's coup, Mrs Doe was what is known as a market woman, who sold fried food in the market to eke out the exiguous wages of a master sergeant. A picture of her at a reception shortly after the coup, standing between her still-slender husband and his father, who is clearly bemused by his sudden change in fortune, shows her as a fine-featured woman with a pleasantly modest expression. Her elevation to the First Ladyhood, however, soon resulted in the same physical coarsening as that undergone by her husband: in Africa, success is rapidly made flesh. She became heavy, and her expression cruel and peremptory. In a ludicrously sycophantic book about Doe compiled by the Liberian Ambassador to London, Willie A. Givens, entitled *Liberia: The Road to Democracy Under the Leadership of Samuel Kanyon Doe*, published by a vanity press, there is a photograph of Mrs Doe with the caption '. . . [her] moral support helped him overcome danger and difficulties'.

It was said that Mrs Doe grew estranged from her husband, who sought compensation elsewhere, and spent much of her time not at the Executive Mansion but in her own house, returning to his side only for official occasions. Thereafter she concentrated on business. She had seen the end coming and tried to persuade her husband to leave Liberia while he was still able, but he stayed and she left for London, where she now lived in comparative penury, deprived of access to her husband's bank accounts.

The house was Third-World *nouveau riche*, an almost styleless square building, but with occasional, stylistically arbitrary, decorative flourishes. It had received a direct hit from a rocket, and at the rear had been almost completely destroyed. This damage, however, was not visible from the front.

The gates were open and I walked in. Under the *porte-cochère* a woman was cooking over a fire made from furniture. She was boiling rice in an iron pot, without anything to accompany it. Nearby was an elaborate table, or rather half an elaborate table, for it had been broken or chopped into two. I suspected that it also would soon be crackling under the pot. Made of nearly white wood, its top was held up by a central support carved in the shape of an enormous goldfish. Although it was done with some skill, the impression was of ineffable vulgarity. (Skill exercised in the service of kitsch is a double misfortune.) Nearby was a chair in the mass-produced sub-Louis-Quinze style, gilded and upholstered and as preposterously out of place as a walrus on a tennis court.

I was greeted with extreme suspicion. The woman doing the cooking said nothing, but looked at me with small, slightly bloodshot eyes. She was soon joined by several other people, all of whom, I gathered, lived in Mrs Doe's former house. Their leader, or spokesman, was a tiny man, not above five feet tall and as sinewy as a whippet. He had a scar on his face and deeply expressionless eyes. He was the only one among them who spoke, and he was not to be mollified by pleasantries.

'Good morning,' I said.

'What are you doing here?' he replied.

By 'here' he clearly meant the house, but I deliberately misunderstood him. I explained my presence in Liberia.

'Where are you from?' he asked.

'London.'

'The BBC?' He spat the letters with venomous hatred. The BBC stood for truth in Liberia, and – in the circumstances – he had no truck with truth.

'No,' I said. I changed the subject abruptly, though

perhaps not deftly. 'Mrs Doe lives in London, doesn't she?'

'You know Nancy?' He seemed eager for news or a message. 'We are her relatives.'

I confessed that I had never actually met her; I did not even know where in London she lived. His hostility, which he had briefly managed to control, surfaced again.

'Why have you come here? This is a private house.'

It *was* a private house, but the cause of his hostility was that he had much to hide and more to fear. His manner convinced me that he had taken part in the massacre at St Peter's church: he lived near his work. For him, every visitor was now (and would be for the rest of his life) an emissary of his enemies, bearing their revenge. He lived in Mrs Doe's house, waiting for Death to ambush him.

I explained as blandly as I could that Mrs Doe was a woman of historic importance, and that any house in which she had lived was therefore of historic importance also. I added that I should like to see inside it.

The little man was evil, but he wasn't stupid. History – or his past – was at the root of his fear.

'It is better you leave now,' he said.

On the whole, I thought he was right: for he was someone who would cut a man's throat as inpassively as a fishwife gutting fish.

11

THE ARMY

The Armed Forces of Liberia, Doe's army, had not been entirely defeated in the civil war. Easily driven out of the rest of the country, they had stood and fought in Monrovia. They never lost their barracks or the area around the Executive Mansion. In the words of Field Marshal Brigadier-General Prince Y. Johnson, Charles Taylor had driven up to the Executive Mansion with his men and then run away again. When the cease-fire was signed, the AFL were left in existence, confined to their barracks and not permitted to wear uniforms (except for the military police) or bear arms. The cease-fire was at best a temporary settlement.

I went twice to the Barclay Training Center, the remaining stronghold of the AFL. Not an impressive institution, it was a large compound built on the seashore, with a long wall running along the beach. I was told that on the other side of the wall, where people were wary of going, it was not difficult to find human remains, scarcely buried in the sand, the AFL being careless or unimaginative in the disposal of the evidence of their activities. To the right as one entered the BTC (as it was universally known) there was a dusty field for sport and square-bashing, with a rickety reviewing stand; to the left, some two-storey administrative offices and the chapel. Behind these were the living quarters for the troops.

153

One could tell if any of the generals was 'on seat', as West-African English puts it, by the presence or absence of expensive new tinted-windowed four-wheel drive vehicles parked outside the offices. Even the generals were not allowed to wear uniforms, however; and an army confined to barracks in civilian clothes, with no arms, and uncertain that it will be permitted to survive as an institution, does not present the appearance of a disciplined force. The vast majority of the soldiers and officers of the AFL were of the Krahn tribe; it was thus an army waiting to be massacred.

The military policeman at the gate searched the car in which I arrived with that mixture of officiousness and insouciance with which minor functionaries perform duties whose purpose (beyond obedience to orders) they do not understand. He accepted without question that I was who I said I was, but insisted upon seeing inside the glove compartment. My driver flashed it open and shut so quickly that, had it contained a grenade or pistol, the military policeman would not have seen it. He waved us on, his duty done.

The soldiers, who were neither demobilized nor on active duty, milled about, apparently with little to do. They displayed no curiosity as to my presence, and they engaged in no animated conversation among themselves. This, I thought, is what Purgatory must be like.

I was taken almost at once to see one of the generals commanding the BTC. His name was Philip B. Kamah, and he worked, or sat, in a darkened office, into which I was shown by a soldier with scruffy clothes but a smart salute. We passed through an antechamber, on whose artificial leather sofas reclined several officers in sneakers, listlessly awaiting orders. It took a little while for my eyes to become accustomed to the gloom of the general's office. This darkness, whether deliberately arranged or not, no doubt

154

gave him the advantage in appraising visitors. There was an electric fan on his desk, but it did not work.

The general was taciturn and suspicious. He regarded even the date and time of day as state secrets to be jealously guarded, and therefore answered none of my questions directly. When I asked how many men there were at the BTC, he replied, 'I know I have soldiers, that is all I know. Yes, I have soldiers.' In talking to me, he had something to lose and nothing to gain. He did, however, grant me permission to walk around the barracks with a couple of his men as guides. Before I left his office he handed me a slim foolscap pamphlet entitled *Armed Forces Day Brochure*. This was printed for Armed Forces Day 1991, when the lion of the Army sat down with the lamb of the Interim Government (there being little alternative for either). A picture of the new Commander-in-Chief, His Excellency Dr Amos C. Sawyer, whom the army had, in Samuel Doe's time, forced into exile, graced the cover. Inside, the interim Minister of National Defense, Dr Edward Binyah Kesselly, sent a message to the AFL: 'Military men and women should always consider it beneath their dignity and honor to be ordered to form death squads in destruction of the lives of the very citizens whose hard taxes are utilized in maintaining the military . . .' The Chief of Staff of the AFL, Lieutenant-General J. Hezekiah Bowen, made a rather different point in his address to the troops: 'On 24 December, 1989, the Army was called to its constitutional duty to defend the peace-loving people of this country against armed incursion brought about by some power-greedy individuals within our society . . .' This seemed to me a somewhat inadequate formulation, both of the problem and of the army's method of dealing with it.

The brochure had photos of the officers of the AFL or,

more accurately, spaces for photographs of them. Those few that did appear were not a good advertisement for the Army: no group of hardened convicts could have looked more sinister. Badly printed as these photographs were, it was possible still to make out the absolute cruelty, the utterly immobile feelinglessness of the features. The pictures of Colonel J. Sackor Gippleh, Commander of the Board of Investigation of the AFL, Amos G. Garlo, Commander of the Military Police, and Second Lieutenant Freddy Q. Pappo, were outstanding in their capacity to produce a shudder. One would have wished for death rather than to fall into their hands. Twenty-seven officers with the rank of colonel or above seemed excessive for a force that could not have numbered more than fifteen hundred.

It was not very long before the two men who accompanied me around the camp sought to persuade me of the poor conditions in which the army lived. Perhaps they knew the sentimental connection in every western liberal's mind between poor living conditions and appalling behaviour. 'Is it any surprise we committed massacres,' they might have asked, 'when we are made to live like this?'

We went behind the barracks to a foetid and shallow little well. This, they said, was where the soldiers had to get their water for cooking, washing and drinking. There was another, similar well a little further away, but that was all. The water was as brown as tea, and there was very little of it. It would have been difficult to scoop up any without at the same time scooping up the underlying mud. I agreed that as a source of water it left much to be desired. Delighted by my reaction, the two plain-clothes soldiers said that sometimes the men at the BTC had almost died of thirst. I found it difficult to believe that soldiers would passively allow themselves to die of thirst for lack of water in the middle of a city, but kept my counsel.

We walked through the barracks themselves. They were plain single-storey concrete houses, not beautiful, but the soldiers seemed proud of them. Before Doe, they said, the non-commissioned soldiers of the Liberian Army had lived in shacks of tin and whatever other materials they could find. In reality, it was the poor conditions of military service as much as an abstract love of social justice that provoked the coup. I asked whether I might see inside one of the houses. There was no one at home in most of them, but a few had women outside washing clothes in a bucket or preparing a fire for cooking. I might have been invisible for all the notice they took of me. We found a house with the door open and asked permission to enter, which was granted by a woman who was neither hostile nor friendly, but who accepted the strange visitation with complete resignation.

It was hot as hell inside, the concrete walls and tin roof of the house capturing the heat and augmenting it. Two families lived in the house, one in each room, and the living space between was so cluttered with furniture and ornaments that it was difficult to move about. The style of the furnishings was tropical-Victorian-kitsch, the preferred colour being the deep wine-red of opera-house plush. There were china cats, glass dogs, plaster birds and plastic flowers everywhere, in the worst of all possible taste, but precious to their owners and therefore worthy of respect.

On a sofa which served also as a bed – the house was so small that everything in it had to serve as several things – a baby lay, obviously unwell. His skin was hot, he was thin and dehydrated. He was probably suffering from malaria, and was so ill that he had passed through fractiousness to apathy. I said to the mother that I was a doctor, but she was as listless as her child. Was this fatalism, superstition or distrust? Perhaps the mother herself was ill and consequently exhausted. I remembered a passage from a book published in 1948 about Liberia, written by an American woman, Esther Warner, who went with her husband to live on the Firestone plantation:

> The mother sat in front of her hut on a bamboo mat, bathing the tiny wrinkled baby in a white-enameled pan. She scooped water in her palm from beside the little clay-daubed body and poured it into the child's mouth.
> 'That child should not drink bath water,' I said in my best child-care-and-training manner.
> 'Only pepper and small medicine to make pickin strong inside the water,' said Ashmanah. 'So our people do every time. Pickin out of that woman can't live.'
> 'The pickin must chop milk from the mother. Bath water is not fit pickin chop.' I knelt on the mat and pushed the child's mouth over the nipple of one of the woman's swollen breasts to be sure they understood. The woman snatched the breast angrily from the child.
> 'Only the water with medicine inside for three days,' said Ashmanah. 'So is the way of our people.'
> 'You make Death the way of your people!'
> 'No,' argued Ashmanah. 'When God say "live", my pickin live . . .'

I turned my eyes to the wall. There was a framed photograph of Samuel Doe there, in the early days of his reign when he sported an Afro haircut like a revolutionary halo, and before (as the poet, politician and sanitary engineer, C. Plato Warner, put it) 'he tasted the pudding and found it sweet'.

'Do you recognize that man?' asked one of the soldiers.
'Of course,' I replied. 'He's Samuel Doe.'
'He's the man we miss,' he said.

I visited the BTC again when General Hezekiah Bowen, Chief of Staff, was interviewed by a Swedish television team. I had conceived the utmost contempt for Scandinavians in Africa ever since my time in Tanzania, where I learnt of their desire to be deceived and to deceive themselves through disregard of the most patent and blindingly obvious realities. It was largely their money which paid for the forcible resettlement of several millions of poor peasants over a period of two years. This was at the instigation of the honey-tongued tyrant Nyerere, who knew how to play upon the Scandinavians' self-congratulatory guilt over their own prosperity as a flautist plays upon a flute. It was largely (though alas not only) the Scandinavians in Africa who granted secular canonization to Nyerere because he did not sleep in a golden bed, even as he produced economic disaster while talking of utopia; it was they who solemnly listened to his secular sermons (while retaining in their innermost being an awareness of their own superiority), and it was their hosannahs that rent the heavens as Nyerere tried to institute a totalitarian regime, failing in his design only because of administrative incompetence and the good-humoured decency of his people. I feared the compassion of the Scandinavians as I feared the cruelty of other peoples; for their compassion was simultaneously neurotic and abstract, sentimental and ruthless. It was, after all, the ultra-caring Swedish economist Gunnar Myrdal who, desperately anxious about the plight of the poor of South Asia, wrote: '... change ... must be attained by resolutely altering the institutions within which people live and work ... But

159

institutions can ordinarily be changed only by resort to what in the region is called compulsion – putting obligations on people and supporting them by force.'

But these Swedes were different. Reality had long since done to their illusions what the touch of a finger does to the blush of a grape. Moreover, they were paying their own way in Liberia, in the hope that they would sell the films they made there to recover their costs. I admired their enterprise; and, unlike so many of the professionally compassionate I have met, they had a keen sense of humour (at least, they laughed at my jokes). And they paid General Bowen the compliment of treating him precisely as they would have treated any other powerful personage, politely but with scepticism for what he said.

We waited a while outside the general's office. A throng of officers in civilian clothes gathered there, some of them pretending to be engaged upon business, papers tucked under their arms, but most of them merely passing the time in obvious idleness. The desultory clatter of an ancient typewriter could be heard issuing from an office; probably a circular to the effect that 'human life was precious and should not be taken without good reason' was being prepared for all the camp notice-boards.

A few of the officers had that deadness of affect which reminded me forcefully of Prince Johnson's deputy, the vice-Field Marshal Samuel G. Varney. Was it terrible experiences that had made them like this, or was it their character which led them to have terrible experiences in the first place? One of them, a man in his early thirties, had a broad scar across his face, the result of some fearful gash, and eyes as dull as stones. When he spoke, no expression invaded his voice; he was neither friendly nor unfriendly, only indifferent to the very depths of his being. For him, all the world was an abattoir.

We were shown into the general's office. By the standards of the bare and chaotic building, it was luxurious, though its carpeting and furnishings were suited to a colder climate than Liberia's, or to air conditioning that worked. The general's desk was wide and large, as were his responsibilities. The only paper on the desk was a letter from the pastor of a church called Christ Temple International, which began 'Dear Brother Bowen'. On the wall facing the desk was a map of Liberia, and a poster of a boy by a dustbin with the words 'De War Fini – War Gabbage'.

The general was bluff and hearty, full of military affability. His gestures were large, his laughter booming. I had heard that he was the least brutal of all the senior officers in the army, and certainly one felt, in talking to him, that he was still in contact with the rest of the human race. He too was in civilian clothes, and if the deprivation of his uniform humiliated him, he did not allow it to show. He welcomed us as if recent times past had been peaceful and he himself were the head of a respected institution.

There were several other officers in the room, the most important among them being Colonel Arthur B. Dennis, author of such works as *The History of Liberian Armed Forces Day* and *Introduction to the Practice of Military Customs: Guide for Civilians*, the latter of which, not without pride, he distributed to us. This little book informs civilians on how they should (or must) behave in the presence of the military. For example, a table near the end of the book prescribes the correct behaviour of 'Civilians not more than seven in Taxi or small car' and of 'Civilians more than seven in buses or big car' should they come across a funeral 'transferring a casket under military honors'. In his concluding comments, the colonel says that 'we have now come to the end of our exercise' – literary square-bashing – and that his readers should now be aware of the military customs that are 'the *sine qua non* of civilians'.

The combination of military punctilio and intense tribal feeling – the blurb of his book mentions that Colonel Dennis is a 'member of the Krahn ethnic group' – was no doubt responsible for some of the worst atrocities of the civil war.

The interview with the General began. The young Swedish woman who conducted it looked frail but was tough and unafraid. She began with easy questions, such as the size of the Army ('brigade size') and its function ('to guard whosoever is President').

Had not that been its function also at the time of the 1980 coup against Tolbert?

General Bowen had not been in Monrovia at the time of the coup, so he could not comment. However, the President (Tolbert) had not been effective, and there had been no possibility of impeaching him.

What was the future role of the Army in Liberia?

'The army is a unique body,' said the general. 'We keep our soldiers abreast of how to interact with civilians.' The soldiers, it seemed, were to be converted into road builders and social workers. He explained how many of his men were already working on carpentry. 'The Army will be oriented to civilian work.'

How did the general explain the predominance of the Krahn tribe in the Army?

He said that there were many non-Krahns in the Army. He himself was of mixed parentage, for his mother was a Gio, while his father had been Krahn (he omitted to mention that tribal membership was patrilineal). 'Besides', he said, 'the Krahn like the Army, they believe in the Army.'

Had not the Army served the interests of the Krahn tribe? 'We were not looking for tribe,' said the general. 'The rebels were looking for tribe. We don't want anything – we want straightness.' As for Taylor, he was a coward who could only fight civilians. If the Army were supplied with logistics, it would 'clear the road in a split second'.

The fact that the Army harboured no political ambitions was demonstrated, according to the general, when it handed over the keys of the Executive Mansion (the presidential palace) to the new Interim Government. At the end of the fighting, the Army had still held the area around the Mansion, but had voluntarily ceded control to President Sawyer. What could be better proof of its good faith?

What about morale in the Army? Surely it was low?

The general referred to conditions in the Army before the coup of 1980. Did we know how much soldiers earned in those days? No, we didn't. Well, it was $33.33 a month. Did we know how much they earned today (though admittedly there was some temporary difficulty in paying them at all)? Again, we didn't. The general announced the figure triumphantly (after consulting Colonel Dennis): $214 a month.

Did he really imagine this constituted an improvement in his men's pay? Either he did, or his imitation of doing so was a very good one. In 1980, the soldiers had been paid in US dollars; now they were paid in 'Doebucks'. If these were converted to US dollars at the prevailing rate of exchange (six Doebucks to the US dollar), the soldiers were now paid $35.66 a month instead of $33.33, a purely numerical increase of seven per cent in ten years. In the meantime, of course, the value of the dollar had fallen, because of inflation, by at least half, and so the soldiers were very much worse off – at least monetarily – than they had been before Doe's coup. Yet the general beamed at the interviewer,

'QED' plainly written on his face.

A general may be ignorant of economics, but surely not of what the soldiers under his command have done. Without a hint of apology or embarrassment, the young Swedish interviewer broached the subject of atrocities. What did the general know of the atrocities committed by his men?

Accusations to this effect, he said, were false, baseless and without foundation. His men had fired back, that was all. The rebels had killed far more people than the Army.

What about Nimba County, where there were well-attested and documented accounts of wholesale terror, looting and rapine?

Nimba County, said the general, was the base from which the rebels operated. It was therefore quite naturally the scene of the heaviest fighting.

And what had the general to say about the massacre in St Peter's Church? I admired the young woman's directness and thanked heaven I was a white man.

The general kept his head under fire, though I could see that not very deep inside he was boiling with rage. He was thinking it was intolerable that he, a general of the Army, an elder of the church and a man old enough to be this frail young woman's father, should have to reply to her arrogant and impertinent questions. What did she know of real life, of hardships and the struggle for existence and for power? Until she had tasted the dregs of life, how dare she sit in judgement on those who had!

But her frailty notwithstanding, she represented something more powerful than the Liberian Army and her questions had therefore to be answered. The general said he had been out of the country when the alleged massacre in St Peter's Church took place, so he was ill-informed upon the subject; but the figure given for the dead was surely much exaggerated. (I had met someone who had counted the bodies when they were first discovered.)

Nevertheless, the general agreed that there had been a massacre in the church?

Yes, but there was no evidence as to who had done it. It could have been rebels dressed up as soldiers to give the Armed Forces of Liberia a bad name. Besides, many of the supposed refugees in the church were, in fact, rebels in disguise. They took refuge by day and fought by night.

The general was untroubled by, or unaware of, the contradictory nature of what he was saying. The idea of rebels disguised as soldiers attacking rebels disguised as refugees might have been amusing, had the matter not been so terrible and tragic. The interviewer did not draw the general's attention to the inconsistency of what he was saying, leaving it to the viewers to arrive at their own conclusions.

The interview was now over. The general, who had shown signs of strain, relaxed back into his jovial, back-slapping mood. Colonel Dennis was waiting to pounce.

'You have asked a lot of questions,' he said. 'Now it is only fair that you should answer ours.'

There were several questions I could think of which might have caused us some embarrassment: had we come to Liberia to further our own careers, did the destruction we found there confirm us in our feelings of cultural superiority, were we enjoying ourselves amidst the ruins, did the level of suffering in Monrovia match up to what we had expected and hoped for, or were we disappointed in it?

Colonel Dennis asked none of these questions; instead, he worried away at the point he wanted to make like a terrier with a rat.

'Why do foreign journalists always call the Armed Forces

of Liberia Doe's army?' he asked indignantly. 'We are not the remnant of Doe's army. We are the constitutionally and legally prescribed armed forces and our job is to defend the constitution. So why do you always call us the remnant of Doe's army?'

It seemed that we could say anything else about the AFL, as far as Colonel Dennis was concerned, for example that it had committed innumerable atrocities, but that to call it the remnant of Doe's army (an apt enough description of it, after all) was a mortal and unforgivable insult. The colonel was a man whose mind fixed immediately and irremovably on to trivial detail, partly perhaps from the military habits of a lifetime, but perhaps also to defend himself from the painful necessity of thinking about more serious matters.

We assured him that we would register and pass on to the world his objection to the Armed Forces of Liberia being called the remnant of Doe's army.

Near the exit from the Barclay Training Center was the chapel, and the Chaplain-General showed us round it. He described how many hundreds of civilians, not all of them of the Krahn tribe, had taken refuge in its cool, wood-panelled interior during the civil war, and how there was still an old man of the Gio tribe who lived there. The Chaplain-General was smooth and bland, unctuous in the manner of chaplains, and did not tell all he knew.

By the entrance to the chapel was a plaque:

THE CHARLOTTE TOLBERT MEMORIAL CHAPEL, BARCLAY
TRAINING CENTER
This Sacred Edifice Was Completed and Dedicated to the
Glory of God and the Service of Man on Sunday 15th
December AD 1985 by Dr. Samuel Kanyon Doe,
Head of State

and Commander-in-Chief, Armed Forces of Liberia.

Was I alone in finding this plaque deeply offensive? Charlotte Tolbert was the mother of the very William R. Tolbert whose throat Doe cut while he was still in his bed, and whose associates he shot like vermin. Perhaps Doe thought he was doing something noble in thus reconciling himself to the family of the man he murdered (it was La Rochefoucauld who said that we never forgive those whom we have wronged). But if murderers are to reconcile themselves to their victims and their victims' families merely by gestures such as the posting of a plaque on a chapel wall, which of us could sleep easy in his bed?

12

THE EXECUTIVE MANSION AND SAMUEL DOE'S JU-JU

I visited West Point, the worst slum in Monrovia. It was overcrowded, but not as overcrowded as it had once been: much of its population fled the civil war, and was only now beginning to return. West Point belonged to no tribe; it was the crucible in which, perhaps, a new Monrovian identity would eventually be forged from the many tribal identities, first melted and then amalgamated in the fires of common poverty and inescapable proximity.

I had seen too many Third-World slums to be greatly shocked by West Point. In any case, I find such slums far less dispiriting and miserable than the slums of my own country, England. Partly it is a matter of the weather: the cold and the damp exert a multiplying effect on the discomforts of penury. Partly it is a matter of the people: in West Point, for example, they were active, flamboyant and busy, but in English slums they are passive and crushed. To survive in West Point is something of an achievement, and a cause for pride; survival in English slums is virtually guaranteed, but there is no other source of self-esteem.

The road through West Point was narrow. On either side were small stores, bars and beauty salons with daydreamt names: Manhattan, Chicago, Paris. The salons had naïve pictures of glamorous women dancing with rich men in evening dress (with bow ties the size and colour of Amazonian butterflies) painted on their walls, precisely the kind of frivolity in the midst of poverty which many *bien-pensant* friends of the poor in rich countries would like to see abolished in favour of virtuous abstinence. In the brave new Africa of the *bien pensant*, who forgive the Africans because they know not what they do, the money formerly spent on hair-dos and frilly dresses will be spent on vaccinations and contraceptives. Everything will be ruled by an allegedly rational calculus of long-term advantage, and pleasure will be postponed for a century or two until the infant mortality rate has declined to 'acceptable' levels. As I observed the vibrant pullulation of small-scale commercial life in West Point, I recalled Macaulay's remark about the puritans and bear-baiting: 'The Puritan hated bear-baiting, not because it gave pain to the bear, but because it gave pleasure to the spectators.'

Still, life in West Point was obviously very hard: I should have found the physical rigours of subsistence there onerous indeed. Even worse was the lack of privacy: the shacks of black wood were so closely packed together that it was difficult to tell where one began and another ended. Even with the population of West Point halved (as I was told it had been by the war), each shack seemed to house at least an extended family or two, with all the attendant noise, smoke, smell and squalor of overcrowded living. Each person's actions must have been visible and audible to a hundred others. Never to be alone – what exquisite torture! I had to remind myself that among some of the peoples I had known, the need to be alone did not exist; indeed, a person expressing such a need was regarded as ill, and worthy of consolation. The judgement of the unhappiness of others by the standard of one's own preferences is full of pitfalls.

Towards the shore, the slum was built on black – or blackened – sand. At every available space between the blocks of shacks were carbon-covered oil drums, used for drying fish over charcoal; the smell of dried fish impregnated everything. The beach itself was indescribable: here the smell of sewage mingled with that of the fish, and rubbish lay as thick as on a municipal tip. Nevertheless, children splashed happily in the water, and fishing canoes lay on the beach, cleaving the litter. In the far distance the Ducor Palace Hotel stood in lonely eminence; nearer by, two palm trees moved their fronds in the breeze, while a small group of boys collectively evacuated their bowels near the shore, unhurried and unembarrassed.

A few people attached themselves to me and followed me round. There was no menace in this: on the contrary, they were notably polite and well-disposed. My companions became my guides, and they took me through the maze of shacks. My unexpected visit called forth the mirth of children and the handshakes of rheumy old women who sat on the step at the entrance to their shacks. I felt safer, by quite a wide margin, than I should have done in a tower block in a slum in England. No doubt the people of West Point might rise now and again to riot in protest against some particularly odious act or omission on the part of the government, but it seemed to me mistaken to conceive of their lives as constant misery and nothing else. Liberators beware! It is possible to make the lives of the poor worse as well as better; indeed, it is much easier to do so. As I walked through West Point, I had tucked under my arm a broadsheet published by Charles Taylor's National Patriotic Front of Liberia which was full of the populist cant which has done so much damage throughout Africa, and which had already played its part in the destruction of Liberia:

171

Anyone who fails to see the struggle of Liberia within the global framework of oppressed people, will definitely not understand why in Liberia today, even after the demise of Samuel Doe, the struggle still continues . . . The mechanism for [the New World Order] began to be put in place when progressive leaders of the Third World were violently replaced by military regimes, when the politics and economics of these countries were placed into the hands of generals and master sergeants, who owed their allegiance, not to the people but rather to the external imperialist government who installed them into power. Yes, the mechanism was finally complete when these countries' economies became locked into the international monetary fund or IMF ironically referred to by many as the 'Infant Mortality Fund'.

The bottom line of his policy is to allow industrial countries un-obstructed access to the raw materials and human resources as well as absolute control of these countries. Yes, this so-called New World Order is a rebirth of colonialism and 20th Century slavery . . . Any Third World country, like Liberia, which seeks to expose the truth behind the 'New Order' and protect the sovereignty, independence and freedom of the people, poses a threat to this neo-colonial policy of industrialized nations. Brothers and sisters, my fellow Liberians, this hypocritical, diabolical, unpatriotic move by misguided mis-educated and non-Afrocentric politicians must serve as an eye-opener for all Liberians . . .

We as Liberians, must own and operate the majority of Businesses in our country. We are qualified, mature and equipped to turn Water Side, Camp Johnson Road, Broad and Benson Streets into business zones with stores owned and operated by Liberians . . . We must liberate our minds, be ourselves, re-write our history and thereby develop an Afro-centric approach to solving our problems.

These are the words, not of a poor man, but of an educated (or semi-educated) *enragé*, who resents the success of foreign traders and thinks that all wealth is the product of theft. For him, the fundamental question of political economy is, Who is to be the thief? The poor are no more than instruments for his self-aggrandizement and it is resentment that he is not one of the élite, rather than compassion for the actual, living poor, that motivates him.

Does anyone believe such rhetoric any more? I met no one in Monrovia who believed that the 'struggle' was about anything other than money and power. When Doe came to power, he said in his first broadcast address to the nation (which he could not, at that time, have written himself):

The April 12th Revolution was regarded by the Liberian people as a heaven-sent blessing and the only means by which they could be liberated from more than a century of oppression and suffering.

Having as its principal objective the building of a New Society based on justice, equality, freedom, equal opportunity and full participation of all in the nation's affairs, the Liberian Revolution is not, in any way, inclined towards the elimination of any element of the population.

Illusion dies hard, but it is not immortal.

In one of the narrow alley-ways of West Point I found some pages from a school exercise book lying on the ground, and I picked them up to see what was written on them. My companions thought this an odd proceeding, but

173

were too polite to say so. The work on the pages, written in a laborious, child-like hand, had been done two years ago, before the war.

ENGLISH NOTES

There are two kinds of Prodicate, the Simple Prodicate and the Expanded Prodicate.
There are four kinds of sentences.

1 Declarative   3 Imperative
2 Interrogative   4 Exclamatory

There followed some exercises in which the pupil struggled painfully with the formal grammatical analysis of several long sentences. His grasp of English was not secure, but the very handwriting – with rounded letters heavily pressed into the paper – spoke eloquently of herculean effort, of a tongue protruding through the lips because of such intense concentration. In these inauspicious surroundings, amidst the overcrowding and poverty of West Point, I found this strenuous (if outwardly absurd) attempt to master an abstract skill of no immediate practical value oddly moving. It indicated a will to transcend an undoubtedly sordid reality, a will notably lacking in British slums, at least among the native-born. In Liberia, the beacon of hope illumined the parts of speech and clause analysis.

But hope of what, exactly? I had long been familiar with the African thirst for education, and had come to both admire and mistrust it. In Tanzania, my subordinates used to ask me for personal loans for their children's school fees (which they always repaid promptly), and I found the willingness to make sacrifices on behalf of their children, when they themselves were so impoverished, impressive indeed. Less laudable, perhaps, was the glorious future they envisaged for their children, which education was intended to bring about. The only *real* work, in their view, was in government bureaucracy: farming and other productive activity was strictly for fools. In a government office, one had influence and security (for government employees never lost their jobs), one had to do very little to earn, that is to say extort, a lot, one could help one's relatives, and one sat in an air-conditioned office instead of breaking one's back with a hand hoe in the broiling sun, trying to raise a miserable crop of maize which, as likely as not, the baboons would harvest. Of all the legacies of colonialism in Africa, this was by far the worst: that it was the duty and function of an educated élite to direct and control the life and activities of society.

Was material advancement through bureaucratic manipulation, then, the ultimate purpose of learning the parts of speech and clause analysis, or was the knowledge valued for its own sake? My head told me the former, my heart the latter; and I believed my heart. The eventual mastery of English was a great joy and consolation to those for whom it was not the mother tongue.

In any case, there were other paths to power and wealth in Liberia, as Samuel Doe had amply demonstrated. Shortly before his elevation to the presidency, still semi-literate and far from fluent in English, he had sold charcoal in his spare time to supplement his master sergeant's pay. He must have been familiar with West Point, but – man of the people though he was – he soon turned his back on it. He moved into the Executive Mansion, and it was to this monument that I too now turned my attention. My time in Monrovia was running short, and I wanted to see inside the building whose occupation was the object of so many ambitions.

The Executive Mansion was the centre of Doe's resistance

to the rebellion against his rule. When it looked as if the rebels must succeed, for they occupied the entire country except the Mansion and its immediate surrounds, the Army unexpectedly held out and drove them back. It was bravery born of desperation. In the uncharitable words of Brigadier-General Field Marshal Prince Y. Johnson, 'Taylor's men came right up to the Executive Mansion and ran away again.' When the cease-fire was arranged, therefore, the Army was still in possession of the Mansion.

As a proof of its new-found loyalty to the constitution, the Army command had handed the 'key' of the Mansion to the new Interim Government, though the Mansion itself remained physically under the occupation of soldiers loyal to Doe's memory. What this meant to the would-be visitor to the Mansion was that he had now to seek permission to enter it not only from the Army Chief-of-Staff, but from the secretary to the President's office. Running the latter official (a former writer of school textbooks on the history of Liberia) to ground proved difficult: in the absence of telephones, I chased round the city after him on the basis of mere rumours of his location. Once I saw his maroon Mercedes heading in the opposite direction from the one in which I and my loyal taxi driver were going; we turned round, tyres squealing, and tried to give chase, as they do in the movies. But the Mercedes was new, whereas our small Toyota was so aged that one could follow its uncertain progress along the road through the rusted holes in its floor; and the secretary, sitting back importantly in the rear of the Mercedes, was waved through the roadblocks whereas we were stopped and searched every time.

Eventually, however, I found him in the Ducor Palace Hotel. My driver said he knew him quite well, having been to school with him, and greeted him in the normal friendly

Liberian fashion, with just a hint of deference for his newly-acquired eminence. The secretary, however, was so preoccupied with pressing public affairs or so overwhelmed with his own importance that he declined to recognize my driver as anything other than a humble petitioner. Perhaps he did not like to be reminded of the social *milieu* from which he sprang. Nevertheless, he wrote something for us on a piece of paper: not the permission itself, but an instruction to another official to give us permission if he considered it right to do so.

I began to despair. My time was running out, and it seemed to me of transcendent importance that I should enter the Executive Mansion. Suppose the next official passed me on to yet another official? Was this a method of refusing permission without actually saying so? Or was I, at some stage, expected to offer money to expedite matters? I needn't have worried. When at last we found him, the official could not have been more obliging. He wrote the permission – on an expensively embossed letterhead left over from the days of Samuel Doe – at once and with a flourish.

We drove without delay to the Executive Mansion. The streets of Monrovia were by now as familiar to me as any in the world, and I had come to love them, ruins and all. I admired the sign painters' pictures on the pockmarked walls of the former video palaces: Marilyn Monroe, Dracula, Charlie Chaplin, Paul Newman, Boris Karloff, Marlon Brando, the Incredible Hulk and Humphrey Bogart, all promiscuously thrown together and depicted with commendable verve. I waved to the roadside booksellers whom I knew well, who sold the speeches of Samuel Doe and the Aphorisms of William V. S. Tubman, edited and compiled by the Reverend J. Bolton Williams. The books were

177

stained by the mould and gecko droppings which are only two of the terrible scourges of reading matter in the tropics. I recognized the street traders and the man whose service to his country consisted of sitting all day with a radio on his lap and turning it up very loud for the BBC World Service news. I should soon be leaving Monrovia, to return to my drab, workaday world, and I felt prematurely nostalgic.

The Executive Mansion is in an area of the city beyond the university, an area set aside for government institutions, all of them more or less damaged or abandoned. They were built in the sixties, when Liberia enjoyed (or at least had) a rate of economic growth second only to Japan's. It was, perhaps, an unfortunate moment in the history of architecture (the Age of Concrete) at which to dispose of more funds for large public buildings than ever before. The Capitol was the first of these buildings, and it is so ugly that it almost transcends mere ugliness. Its central rotunda, with a vast blue saucer for a roof, looks like a Bulgarian commissar's attempt to design a modern airport control tower. With its terrible and brutal confusion of geometric shapes, it is a powerful reminder that in architecture, as in all other arts, modernity is the most transient of qualities. Here, alas, was one place where the civil war was less destructive than it ought to have been.

The Temple of Justice is a concrete tombstone with a few arbitrary projections. Le Corbusier would have approved: a law court is a machine for trying people in. Yet concrete is the architectural antithesis of justice: it is a splendid material for the construction of torture chambers and underground bunkers for governments at war but, when it is left uncovered above ground, it is good for little else.

The Temple of Justice was deserted, but it was not as

178

badly damaged as the Ministry of Foreign Affairs, another tombstone office block, whose every window had been smashed. Here, a question rose irresistibly to the mind: what did a nation of two and a half millions (before a quarter of the population fled over the borders) need with so large a foreign ministry? Could Liberia's trade or strategic interests possibly have justified ten floors of offices? The answer, I surmise, is that there were always a lot of political debts to pay in Liberia, whatever government was in power, and the creation of bureaucratic sinecures, especially in the glamorous field of foreign affairs, was one way to pay them. The windows were smashed by those who were unjustly denied a sinecure.

Ugly as all these buildings are, President Tubman was understandably proud of them:

> Public buildings are very important. They give expression to the aesthetic taste of a community. They speak as well as language of what the people stand for. Shabby buildings, erected in any place, are of no use. When people enter such buildings they do not think much of those who put them up.
>
> When I took office all the foreign newspapers said Liberia was a place of tin-pan shanties, unfinished structures, and that all Government offices were housed in rented buildings. I tried to correct that. With the support of the Legislature we decided to proceed according to the constitutional rank of the different Departments of Government . . . Then, those who had scandalized and criticized us for not having buildings said we wasted money on public buildings. They were so vicious and wicked as to write that enough fufu could be cooked in the kitchen of the Executive Mansion to feed all of Africa . . . I am very

179

happy about what has been done. There is nothing they can say that will change me. I am very happy to know that the Executive Mansion, the Capitol building and the Temple of Justice are as good as any such buildings in the world. And if our detractors do not like it, if they are jealous, or if they hate us because we are black people, let them tear themselves to pieces and go to pot . . .

Alas, President Tubman was at several points misled. A prickly sensitivity to foreign criticism, allied to xenophobia, is not a sound basis for aesthetic judgement. The style of architecture which had evolved in Liberia by 1944 (the year of Tubman's accession), derived from the southern states of America, was by no means devoid of charm. It respected the climate, it was distinctive and unselfconscious, and it avoided the megalomanic gigantism which – so incommensurate with the scale of the society from which it emerged – would have been funny had it not been so unpleasant. Tubman should have had the self-confidence to tell the foreign critics to go to pot before, not after, he engaged foreign architects.

The old Executive Mansion (rented from a private owner) was both grand and accessible, a plain three-storey house with verandahs surrounding all three floors, supported by pillars painted white. It gave directly out on to the street, through a small but lush garden. It belonged to the era when presidents might visit their mothers without driving in a bullet-proof car to the accompaniment of wailing sirens, blue flashing lights and the roar of police motor bike outriders wearing sunglasses and stiff white leather gauntlets.

The new Executive Mansion is large without grandeur and expensive without taste. It is a rectangular block, bent

180

into a slight curve and divided vertically into twenty sections by dark metal girders. Each of these sections is itself divided by a series of metal slats, so that the windows behind are invisible from the outside. Even the number of floors is not discernible from the exterior, so that the impression is created, no doubt correctly, that something discreditable is occurring within which must be hidden from the public gaze. The Mansion cost $15,000,000 to build, at a time when the entire national budget was $27,000,000 a year. Tubman directed the architect that the new mansion 'should be awesome'. When it was completed, Tubman said with girlish modesty, 'It is too good for me to live in, but not too good for a President of Liberia.'

The Mansion looks not like a residence, but like the headquarters of a minor special agency of the United Nations, devoted, perhaps, to the preservation of whales or the regulation of journalism. One could easily imagine hundreds of bureaucrats within its walls passing earnest memoranda and protocols to each other, while whaling vessels prowled the waters of the ocean unimpeded, to the rear of the building.

As we approached the gate (in Tubman's time there was no wall around the Mansion, which gave it more than ever the appearance of an office block), a soldier stepped forward to examine our papers. He was one of Doe's soldiers, a veteran of the Army's last stand. I had inserted a dash of forty Liberian dollars inside the papers which, even with full written permission from the Secretary for Presidential Affairs, was the real *sine qua non* of entry into the Mansion: the soldier examined the money, not the papers, and waved us through with one hand while deftly insinuating the money into his breast pocket with the other.

We entered the Mansion by the tradesmen's entrance, not

through the totalitarian-style *porte-cochère*. This, supported by four immense concrete pillars, was six storeys high, and had a pompous raised concrete driveway sweeping towards it. The tradesman's entrance, by contrast, was at the side of the building, and opened into a kind of basement, but above ground level. There was a long corridor of offices, unoccupied but also unlooted. Slogans were posted on the doors of a couple of them: 'The Struggle Continues' and 'Prevent Beach Erosion'. Loitering in the corridor, with nothing to do but wait for catastrophe and violent death, were a few former soldiers, most of them wearing a T-shirt with a medallion portrait of the late Doe and the words:

President Doe
1980–1990
Congratulations
For Your 10th
Anniversary
From
Ministry of Finance

written underneath. (It would be possible, very nearly, to write the history of the Liberian civil war in T-shirt slogans, which the BBC stringer, Scott Stearns, had assiduously collected.)

The former soldiers regarded me with scarcely disguised hostility. I thought they had a haunted look, and I discerned a feral guilt in their eyes: the guilt of men who, having committed a great crime, are forced to resort to further great crimes merely to cover up the first. Their eyes darted nervously about, as if the humblest object might rise up in accusation against them if looked at too long; and clearly they believed that a stranger – any stranger – might have been sent to be the instrument of a justified retribution. I

182

toured the Executive Mansion under the escort of two of them. We ascended, via a dark stair well that might have been a fire escape in the offices of a ministry rather than the stairs of a grand residence, to the floor above. In the vast entrance hall – which, despite the circumambient heat, gave an impression of frigidity – there was a large and conventional wooden carving of Christ.

There were ex-soldiers on every floor, and they were hostile not only to me but to each other. They looked to their fellows, not for comfort or solidarity, but for betrayal.

We went upstairs to the banqueting hall and ballroom. It was a room such as an *arriviste* family might wish to hold a wedding in, to display their new-found wealth to the world. The décor was mass-produced Louis Quinze; the gilded chairs with oval upholstered backs and spindly legs were made in Paris by a firm called Berthier. Only the president's chair, at the head table, had arms: the other chairs must have been most uncomfortable for Africans of the banquet-attending class, who incline to corpulence, to sit upon for any length of time.

Tipped over on the ground were a couple of huge candelabra, elaborately but crudely carved from cheap wood in which cracks had appeared. The candelabra had been made by someone who wished to produce an effect of grandeur, but had not the patience or the skill to do so. The chief glory of the banqueting hall, however, was its ceiling: completely mirrored. I was uncertain whether to blame the architect or President Tubman for this stroke of vulgarity, but the whole room was an uneasy marriage of ersatz eighteenth-century elegance and 1960s modernity: a Versailles in the sky.

The large hall in which ambassadors were received (in the days when there *were* ambassadors to receive) was likewise of mixed metaphorical décor. There were the same sub-Louis Quinze chairs, though more sturdy, as well as carved Chinese coffee tables painted with birds and dragons. The walls were cream (disfigured by dirty fingermarks), with gilded mouldings. The carpet was deep-piled, a redundant luxury in such a climate except when the air conditioning is turned up so high, for reasons of prestige, that one is obliged to wear warm clothing. (The more important the person in Africa, the colder his air conditioning.) The carpet had been damaged and then crudely repaired by means of patches attached with large stitches and no regard to the original pattern. Now that the air conditioning was no longer working, a mustiness seeped from everything, from the walls, the carpet, the upholstery; a mustiness familiar to all who have stayed in modern African hotels, which depend for their ventilation not upon nature and open windows but upon technology and sealed windows.

In the antechamber to the hall were portraits in oils of Tubman, his wife and the late Doe. Presumably there had once been a portrait of Tolbert, but it had been taken down. Tubman was in tails, Mrs Tubman in an apple green satin evening dress, and Doe in army uniform – a very American uniform. The paintings were done with a crude realism, in vividly primary colours and with bright backgrounds, reminiscent of the advertising art of the 1950s. One cannot look for long at death or the sun, said La Rochefoucauld: or, he might have added nowadays, at a portrait of a Liberian president or his wife.

We went to the Presidential suite of offices. They were dark and wood-panelled, like the offices of important lawyers, and had been ransacked. Many had pictures of Doe – some in a double-breasted suit with matching silk tie and handkerchief, others in Mandingo robes, yet others in

184

uniform – lying on the floor or propped against the wall, face inwards. The text – used by Doe himself – of a speech lay upon a desk; in it, he called for the maximum efforts of businessmen in these times of difficulty. On another desk I found a scroll and the insignia of the Liberian Humane Order of African Redemption. Major-General Henry Y. Jack had been about to be invested as a Knight Commander of the Order, and the award awaited only Samuel Doe's signature for completion. The war, alas, had intervened, and Major-General Jack (whose photograph appears in the Army Day brochure as Commandant of the Tubman Military Academy) would now never be a Knight Commander.

I picked up the dark bronze medal, attached to a red, white and blue ribbon. The Humane Order of African Redemption was founded in the 1870s in imitation of European decorations, when slavery still existed in Brazil and Cuba, and had been abolished for less than ten years in the United States. When it was founded, it expressed what must have been a deep and heartfelt aspiration; by 1990, it was an absurdity (or worse), used by one villain to confer distinction on another.

Next to the scroll and insignia was a letter from an indignant Canadian resident of Liberia, dated 13 May 1990.

> Dear President Doe,
>
> At this time I am registering a vigorous protest against the illegal invasion and occupation of the Republic of Panama! I protest the illegal kidnapping and imprisonment of General Manuel Antonio Noriega.

Why do people write such letters? Why do they work themselves up into a lather about distant events when catastrophe is so close at hand? As I thought of the deeply and drearily conventional mind that had produced this protest, a great weariness overcame me. Men sometimes are like mice which, under the imminent threat of extinction, sit and wash their paws by way of distraction.

We finally reached Doe's inner sanctum, the office of the President. It too was wood-panelled, apart from the large window behind his desk which overlooked the ocean. The desk, I was told, was a replacement for the one that had been looted shortly after his demise. There was nothing in the room to suggest his personality, except perhaps the library globe. This was already familiar to me from a photograph serving as the frontispiece to a heavy blue tome of Doe's speeches, expensively published in London by a vanity press and exported to Liberia, where it was now for sale on street corners for next to nothing. In the photograph, Doe stands in the ambassadors' hall, with two Liberian flags draped from standards behind him. The patterned carpet is beneath his feet, which are slightly apart: the woven word LIBERIA appears just in front of them.

But it is not only Liberia which lies, metaphorically, at his feet. Dressed in an expensive double breasted suit, with loudly matching silk tie and breast-pocket handkerchief, he stares straight into the camera while his right arm rests lightly but proprietorially on the library globe, as if he were the demiurge of the earth's rotation. When I first saw this official photograph of Dr Samuel K. Doe (as the caption calls him), I thought immediately of the scene in Charlie Chaplin's film *The Great Dictator*, in which Adenoid Hinkel plays contemptuously with a balloon painted like the world. At first sight, the photograph of Doe betrays a startling arrogance; but the anxiety and uncertainty underlying his bluster is not hard to detect. Every pompous symbol, every prop, speaks eloquently of a longing to be taken seriously, but also of a fear that, secretly, everyone is laughing at him.

This fear spurs him to ever greater grandiosity which, however, inflames his fears rather than assuages them. (Anyone who has, through nervousness, spoken too much at a social gathering will recognize and understand the vicious circle: having said something foolish, one feels impelled to elaborate on it to retrieve a situation which, however, is only made worse by one's prattle.) Doe was undoubtedly a bad man, but his vices were small and ordinary, made large and significant by power: fear, greed and vanity.

My tour of the Executive Mansion was now over: I was not permitted to see the presidential boudoir, which I had been assured was well worth a visit. There, new heights of vulgarity had been effortlessly scaled. I went instead to Doe's weekend house in Paynesville, guided by my faithful driver who by now knew my tastes in sight-seeing. Doe's suburban villa was to be the last sight I saw in Liberia.

Paynesville illustrates well that shortage of land is not one of Liberia's problems. Although counted part of the city, its houses are scattered, and the plots on which they are built seem barely to be holding the bush at bay. This middle-class suburb would be considered deeply rural in a country such as Holland. Doe's house was down an unpaved and rutted lane which in the rains must have turned to impenetrable mud the colour of goulash. My driver had a relative whose ramshackle house was near Doe's: he was a senior civil servant who formerly kept chickens and pigs to supplement his salary. The chickens and the pigs, however, had departed as surely as the captains and the kings, looted by marauding soldiers. The deserted pigpens and chicken coops presented a melancholy aspect, but the civil servant was planning to start up his business again. His resilience and good humour were admirable.

187

Doe's weekend villa was completely deserted. It was not extravagantly large, and was built in the styleless style of modern middle-class homes throughout the Third World: rectangular concrete boxes placed on top of and at angles to one another. The garden was scarcely large enough to have an orgy in: clearly Doe had had enough of outdoor life as a master sergeant, when he sold charcoal in the market.

At the time of his overthrow and death, the villa was undergoing renovation. To judge from the work that had already been done, and from the long brass-coloured strips of metal that lay still unused upon the ground, Doe's taste was that of a magpie or jackdaw: he liked bright, shiny things. It was a house of coppery mirrors and spangled tiles; had it been furnished, it would have been with white leatherette chairs and pink carpets. Here were the dreams of luxury of a man for whom high intellect meant *Time* and sophistication meant Black Label. I remembered the thousands of people who had died that Doe might continue to live out his vulgar fantasies.

'The late Doe, he like this house too much,' said my driver. 'He come here every weekend.'

'And Mrs Doe?' I asked.

'Ah, no Nancy at weekend. She go for other house.' He smiled knowingly. There had been orgies, he said.

We walked through Doe's deserted weekend retreat. It was undamaged, like the *Marie Celeste*. I remarked to my driver that I found it strange that valuable building materials had been left untouched.

'They are afraiding,' he said, referring to potential looters. 'This house used for Doe's ju-ju.'

'But his ju-ju wasn't very effective, was it?'

He laughed.

'Johnson, his ju-ju was very better.'

13

SIERRA LEONE

A city without water, electricity, sanitation, post office, telephones, newspapers or cultural amenities: surely anyone would be relieved to depart such a place? Yet when it was time for me to do so, I was far from eager. My regret at leaving Monrovia caused me a certain unease: how was it possible that I had enjoyed so thoroughly my sojourn in a city destroyed, a city in which no one knew where all his relatives were, or even whether they were still alive?

In part it was the isolation from my previous existence that I savoured. To arrive in a distant country, without contacts of any kind and without the possibility of communicating with home in the event of distress, is to indulge for a moment in the fantasy that one can start life anew, that the squalid compromises and outright sins of one's previous life now count for nothing. And when, in addition to this, the distant country has been the scene of a desperate civil war, one's absorption in the country's affairs is so overwhelming that self-transcendence is for a time complete.

I was told before I arrived in Liberia that Liberians were inclined to arrogance, that in spite of having brought about a catastrophe, they were convinced that they had conducted themselves creditably. I did not encounter such arrogance, except perhaps among the returning politicians who gathered in the capital like vultures around a carcass. It never occurred to the politicians that the whole sorry situation had anything to do with them; but there was nothing specifically Liberian about their blindness. Nor was there anything specifically Liberian about their inclination to blame others for their plight. They blamed the Americans for removing Tolbert from power because he had established closer relations with the Soviet Union, for supplying Doe with unprecedented quantities of military aid even as he committed terrible atrocities, for pretending that the elections he held in 1985 were other than blatantly fraudulent, for not intervening in the civil war, to which they could have put an end with three hundred marines; they blamed the Libyans, the Ivorians and the Burkinabe for supplying and succouring Taylor; they blamed the Europeans and the Japanese for not offering at once to rebuild the country with aid; they blamed the Lebanese traders for exploiting the commercial possibilities of whatever situation arose; and they blamed just those Liberian tribes to which, by happy coincidence, they did not themselves belong.

Personally, then, I did not encounter anything to justify the ill-repute of the Liberians, so casually imparted to me before my journey. If it is true that a people gets the government it deserves, I suppose it must also be true that it gets the civil war it deserves; but I have yet to meet a people as bad or as vicious as the governments I have met with all round the world. What people, indeed, could deserve a Pol Pot or a Mengistu? Sometimes, I suspect there is an inverse relationship between the qualities of government and people: the worse the government, the better the people. It is true that I met evil men in Liberia: but where would I not meet them?

Flights to Sierra Leone and Gambia had resumed from

Spriggs-Payne Airfield. Schedules were – perhaps flexible is the word I seek. I arrived on time and waited for hours, long enough to indulge in a little premature nostalgia for Monrovia. There was time also to read *Fanon: In Search of the African Revolution*, a volume I had rescued from mouldering decay on a bookstand at Port Harcourt airport in Nigeria on my journey out to Liberia. It was written by a Nigerian political scientist trained in America; it did not increase my enthusiasm for finding the African Revolution.

A Belgian nun *en route* for Sierra Leone was told that she would have to return to Monrovia to obtain an exit visa, a curious formality in a country from which a quarter of the population had already expatriated itself. She pleaded with the official, who relented as much from boredom, and exhaustion, as from kindheartedness. I asked her whether she knew two Irish nuns whom it had been my original plan to visit. They were doctors who ran a leprosarium in the north-east of Liberia which had been overrun first by the Army and then by Taylor's faction. By all accounts, they had had to hide in a cupboard while the battle raged; when it abated, they came out and resumed their care of the lepers, who were otherwise friendless. This was a story that moved me even in barest outline: whenever I defend the possibility of true altruism against the cynics who say that it is but the self-love of psychologically-damaged people, I cite the work of nuns in Africa. But the Belgian nun did not know of the Irish nuns, who were of a different holy order, and now – to my regret – I should never meet them, never go to the town in northern Ivory Coast and ask for the shadowy and crooked representative of Taylor's movement there, who would offer to take me into Liberia for $1000, which I would reject and beat down to $50.

I had bought a ticket to Gambia, but as we boarded the

plane we were told that the flight would now go only as far as Freetown in Sierra Leone. Inwardly, deep in all my viscera, I groaned; Sierra Leone was another country of ill-repute, and I had no entry visa. I spent the flight imagining unedifying scenes at the airport. I needn't have worried. When a country is as near to bankruptcy as Sierra Leone was, bribes are quite reasonably sized, at least for foreigners, and they impart efficiency to even the most sluggish of bureaucrats.

The city was at some distance from its airport, and separated from it by a wide estuary. The fuel crisis (if a crisis can be a near-permanent condition) meant that ferries were infrequent: never mind, the shore of the estuary was a pleasant enough vantage point from which to watch the sun go down, streaking the sky with exotic tropical colours. With the extinction of day, however, the lights of the city on the far shore did not come on. An Indian trader who sat next to me on the bus explained why.

'There has been no electricity or water in Freetown for five years.'

I recalled the large photograph of His Excellency Major-General Dr J. S. Momoh, President of Sierra Leone, which oversaw – at a slight angle – the infrequent comings and goings at the airport. His Excellency's rounded, fleshy countenance stretched his skin until it shone with a glossy, satin sheen. He exuded prosperous well-being almost as a physical secretion: a well-being whose ultimate source, was control over governmental prerogatives such as the granting of import and export licences, and which was not entirely unconnected with the capital's lack of electricity and water. His dictum, where the Sierra Leonean economy was concerned, might well have been Lenin's with regard to the Russian famine of 1891: the worse the better. Certainly, sterling progress had been made in the direction of the worse.

The city, close up, was not entirely in darkness, however; there were glimmerings of kerosene lamps at the side of the road, by the feeble yellow light of which petty traders sold their wares, fragmented into the tiny quantities their customers could afford. One sensed movement in the streets rather than actually saw it. The hotel, it transpired, had an ancient generator of its own, which converted diesel first into noise and only second, a by-product as it were, into electricity.

The hotel was the haunt of various refugees from Liberia seeking a meal. One of them was a Nigerian physician, long resident in Liberia until the civil war compelled him to flee. He tried to pass off an arm injury as the result of torture, but another Liberian informed me that he was a notorious drunk who had fallen down the stairs. I do not think my fellow-doctor was lying, exactly: memory itself alters with the repetition of a story. Unable to sleep, I went for a walk in the dark city. Even the presidential palace opposite the hotel was without light; the President had decamped to a house with its own generator.

I reached the city's and the country's main hospital, and decided to enter. It, too, had no electricity, but was illuminated – if that is the term – by flickering lamps which cast dancing shadows. These lamps imparted the colour of jaundice to everything, creating an effect much gloomier than mere darkness. But the hospital was not as bad as I had expected – and, perhaps, had hoped. There were no dramatic passages to be written about it, no revelations to be made that would stir the conscience of the world. If there were squalor and misery here, it was quotidian. The wards were oven-hot and crowded, and felt like the inside of an incu-

193

bator in a bacteriological laboratory, but there was only one patient to a bed, a ratio by no means to be taken for granted; and while the equipment was antiquated and rusting, it worked after a fashion. I had seen worse, and not only in Liberia; nevertheless, I resolved not to fall ill in Sierra Leone.

The morning dawned bright, hot and humid. When I walked out, I found little groups of pedestrians huddled round men with transistor radios, all listening intently. There were reports on the BBC of armed incursions from Liberia into Sierra Leone by Taylor's men. Taylor's strategy, it seemed, was to spread chaos into the neighbouring countries which were already on the verge of it. I couldn't tell whether the people listening to the reports were elated by them (was this the beginning of the end for His Excellency?) or whether they were frightened by them; certainly, there was tension in the air. Sierra Leone, according to received wisdom, was tinder awaiting its spark; perhaps this was it.

A small convoy of Land Rovers emerged from the gates of the presidential palace, lights flashing, sirens screaming and automatics bristling from the windows in every direction, fending off attacks even from the sky. One might have supposed that the fate of the country hung upon the urgent arrival of the vehicles and their passengers somewhere, were it not that such urgency was as much a sign of self-importance as of importance. The people in the street, habituated to the fuss, did not even turn to look, their indifference as if to say 'It's only them, playing their games – let them if they want to'. The Sierra Leonean uprising, revolution, or what you will, was evidently some way off.

I was approached by a boy who offered me a book for sale. It was called *Once Upon a Time . . . Sierra Leone and a*

President Called Siaka Stevens; it was a comic-strip biography, printed in France, of the man who set his country firmly on the downward spiral. The boy, whose offer was purely speculative, was astonished and delighted that I should want the book, for it contained little but half-truths, lies and evasions. That, of course, was precisely why I wanted it.

I was familiar with this biographical genre from Libreville in Gabon, where – to my subsequent everlasting regret – I failed to buy a similar work about its President, El Haj Omar (formerly Jean-Bernard) Bongo. The two presidents had much in common: auspicious birth, precocious leadership qualities, academic prowess, tactically brilliant struggle against the colonial power, elevation to the presidency by popular acclaim (if not quite by the ballot box) and finally, world importance. Both are family men; they love, and are loved by, children. In the biography of Siaka Stevens there is even a touching scene in which the people, including children, demonstrate before State House with banners demanding a one-party state.

I read this Whig interpretation of Sierra Leone's slide into chaos and poverty on my way to the central post office, the only place in the country, I was told, from which it was possible to communicate with the outside world. There in the boiling telegraph office, half the population of the city seemed to be trying to do so, each of the desperate would-be senders of telegrams drawing the attention of the telegraph clerk behind the counter to his plight by waving a paper, shouting, protesting, pushing and gesticulating (insofar as space allowed). I very nearly despaired at the sight of it, but I should have been mistaken to do so.

My appearance at the office produced a curious calming effect: I was let through almost at once to the counter, where the clerk took down my message for relay to Europe without any *quid pro quo*. It was as if, from a certain delicacy of feeling, no one in the office expected me to take part in that heaving, seething struggle of each against all. It was kindness, servility and recognition of the white man's frailty in Africa, all at once. To my surprise, my telegram reached its destination.

A Liberian refugee had arranged to meet me later in the morning to take me to his refugee camp. He was a young man who wanted to return to Liberia: there was nothing for him in Sierra Leone, he said, only suspicion and hostility. And now that Taylor's men had crossed into Sierra Leone, it was a heaven-sent opportunity for His Excellency the Major-General to divert public attention away from the deficiencies of his regime. The newspapers (under government control, it goes without saying) were already whipping up hysteria about Liberian refugees, claiming that many of them were not refugees at all, but Taylor's agents sent to sow discord among the naturally harmonious Sierra Leoneans. Unfortunately, some of the Liberians, anxious on arrival in their country of refuge to portray themselves as not being of the common herd, had boasted openly of connections with Taylor. This boast, though not believed at the time, had also not been forgotten; and now it was being broadcast – as if it were a recent discovery – to create an artificial solidarity with the government.

The camp was a few miles out of the city, in a dry and arid valley. It was half an hour's walk from the road, and on the way my young companion told me of the fear in which the Liberians now lived. The police often demanded to see their documents; the amount one had to pay the police depended on whether they were in order or not. People were beginning to disappear without trace, he said, and he showed me the latest edition of one newspaper, in which there were photographs of various Liberians who had been arrested overnight as agitators. One of them was the camp nurse, the refugees' only source of medical succour. What were they going to do without him?

The camp was in a disused borstal, whose buildings had never been elaborate and were now virtually ruined. I arrived as the midday meal was served in the open air: plain boiled rice doled out in glutinous lumps (which the flies at least found appetising) from chipped enamel buckets, courtesy of the Red Cross. Supplies were inadequate, the refugees said; it was a long time since they had had anything to accompany their rice and the portions (which came with the burnt skin scraped from the bottom of the pot in which the rice was cooked) were growing smaller by the day. For all that, the refugees did not appear ill-fed to me, and some of the men were notably strapping.

But they were without hope. I went into one of the dormitories – it had served the same function in the borstal days – and found refugees packed like sardines on the floor there, with hardly an inch in which to move, lying listlessly. My appearance did not interest them: they probably thought I was yet another official who had arrived in an air-conditioned, tinted-windowed, four-wheel drive vehicle with quadraphonic stereo, to check that they were not actually dying.

There was a communal hall, where the delinquents, no doubt, had once put on theatrical performances and listened to reformatory sermons. It was empty, apart from an alert old lady in her seventies and her family who had made it their home. A great-grandchild on a mat gave vent to all the excretions that flesh is heir to while she described how she and her family had fled the war, how hard it had been for her with her arthritis to trek through the bush.

197

'No one care for us,' she said, her rheumy eyes looking into mine.

She knew about the latest developments (I suppose rumour travels fast in a refugee camp) and she said that everyone was now afraid that the local residents, who had always been unfriendly and suspicious, would attack them. They were jealous, the old lady said, even of the refugees' free rice, little enough though it was. Why, they asked, should strangers be given food for nothing when it was difficult to find even with hard work? Everyone in the camp now wanted to return to Liberia, rather than continue to live in idleness and fear of reprisal. They had heard that peace had returned to Monrovia, and it was there they wished to go; unfortunately, though the passage cost only ten dollars, they had not the means to do so.

'Tell the world about our situation,' she said, and I promised that I would, as best I could.

'Good', she said, evidently believing that if only the world knew, something would be done. But the world has much to preoccupy it. A small West African country torn by civil war, with half its population displaced and a quarter expatriated, is of less account in the world's eyes than the New Look in Milan, or the divorce of a former Wimbledon champion. And if it is tragedies the world wants, there are worse tragedies than that of the displaced Liberians. Even the killing, by the standards of our century, was small-scale and low-tech. When I agreed to tell the world, I knew that I was fostering an illusory, if merely momentary, hope.

I left Sierra Leone next day by the flight to London. It was one of the last such flights, I was told, there being little passenger demand for the route, which was soon to be abandoned. Naturally there was a long delay and, as a last resort, the English would-be passengers began to talk to one another. I found myself next to an educationist on one side and a family planning expert on the other. Both had come to persuade the Sierra Leoneans to change their ways, but had failed to do so. They ascribed their failure, in part, to the brevity of their visits; for the sake of discussion, I wondered whether their failure resided at a rather deeper level, whether indeed their whole project of reformation of the Sierra Leonean character was not fundamentally misconceived. If everyone were educated, for example, would there be enough office jobs to meet the demand for them, and who would hoe the fields? As for family planning, did not the expense of one video machine equal that of several thousand condoms? Were experts ever needed to induce people to watch videos?

In the duty-free shop, I found something that I thought my interlocutors ought to see and upon the meaning of which they might reflect. We are most of us aware, I suppose, of the difference between Johnnie Walker Red Label and Black Label whisky, in social cachet if not in taste; but how many of us know that there is a Blue Label as well, very rare and very old, and that it sells in the duty-free shop at Freetown airport for one hundred and fifty dollars a bottle, while the city remains in darkness?

ENVOI

I returned to England. Shortly thereafter, I went to Venice for a few days. Beauty, however, does not inspire me like civil war; in the face of it I resort to cliché, and such powers of description as I have fade into embarrassed silence. Since my greatest desire is to write, I have come almost to fear beauty and the wordlessness it provokes in me; but Venice is so completely without parallel, so hauntingly exquisite, that its spell is irresistible even to me. To spend time elsewhere seems a waste of life; one can only console oneself with the thought that, just as happiness is inconceivable without sorrow and suffering, so the ugliness of the world is a necessary preparation for the appreciation of Venice.

As I lingered one Sunday morning, *en route* for the Accademia, outside the Gritti Palace – in which, unfortunately, I was not staying – I happened to look up at the lintel of a nearby *palazzo*, and there, to my intense surprise, was the familiar coat of arms of the Republic of Liberia: a wheelbarrow, hand hoe, palm tree, seagull and sailing vessel just beyond the shore. A brass plate announced that it was the consulate of Liberia in Venice.

Sunday morning is not the hour of diplomatic business, least of all in Venice, and I resolved to call the following day. I rang the bell and a voice, clearly surprised at the interruption to the day's normal inactivity, asked through the entryphone who it was and what was wanted. I explained that I was English and had recently been to Liberia; I wanted to speak to the consul.

A few moments later one of the double doors opened and a grave and ceremonious Italian in his thirties asked me to enter.

'The consul will see you,' he said, and asked me to follow him up some dark stairs. I was shown into a waiting room with barely opened shutters and brown leather chairs reminiscent of a London club fallen (as many of them have) on hard times. The consul's assistant went into the consul's inner sanctum, and then returned to announce me.

The Liberian consul in Venice was an elderly and distinguished Italian gentleman who sat behind a large desk with a small Liberian flag planted upon it, and with a large Liberian flag on a stand behind his right shoulder. On the walls were memorabilia of Liberia. The perfection of the consul's manners made me feel like a northern barbarian.

I explained that I was writing a book about Liberia and that I was interested in his view of the present situation. The consul shook his head sadly. He knew only that it was very bad, but nothing specific: he had had no communication with Monrovia for more than six months. Far from being able to provide me with information, he asked me for whatever news I had.

His assistant stood respectfully on the consul's left hand as he spoke, but as I recounted what I knew he leant forward with the intensity of his concentration. Both of them gave the impression of deep and real concern for Liberia; they were in the employ of a country for which they had a romantic affection. When I had finished my brief description of the ruins of Monrovia, the consul, with evident emotion, recounted his one visit there, before the civil war. It was a happy and beautiful city, he said, and gave no intimation of the savagery to come.

I asked him when, in his opinion, the trouble began. His reply was surprisingly definite, and required no pause for thought.

'In Tolbert's time,' he said. 'That was when the corruption started. Everything was bought and sold.'

The consul was in a good position to know. He had been consul for many years and was accredited in Trieste also. Contrary to appearances now he had once been very busy, on account of the vast merchant fleet which flew the Liberian flag to evade the regulations of more demanding countries. Tolbert had ruined everything by his greed.

I left the consul and his assistant to their melancholy idleness. How odd, I thought on my way to Santa Maria della Salute (the church built to give thanks to God for the passing of the plague in the 1630s which had just killed a third of Venice's population – a strange occasion for gratitude when you come to consider it), that the Liberian officials whom I met who were most obviously concerned with the fate of Liberia were to be found in Venice rather than Monrovia.

I returned once more to England. Language and culture have long made England a place of refuge for Liberians, second only to the United States, and I thought to complete my book by an interview with a prominent exile. To this end, I searched out the address of Mrs Nancy Doe, who lives in Merton in South London, and wrote to her. I was told that she was extremely wary of interviews, having experienced at first hand, and to her cost, the unanswerable power of the press; I promised to be faithful to whatever she said, and to give her a fair hearing.

She did not reply. I obtained her telephone number and rang it. A man with one of those deep, booming West African voices answered. In the background there was an extended family hubbub such as one might hear in any West African town or village: an unexpected confirmation of Horace's dictum that they change their sky, not their soul, who run across the sea.

I explained what I wanted. Again I promised to be fair – a promise which I should not have found entirely reassuring, had our positions been reversed. Without consulting Mrs Doe, the man with the bass voice said:

'I don't think an interview will be necessary.'

There was an unmistakable finality in his diction that brooked no appeal. Further discussion was pointless and, after thanking him, I rang off.

I tried one last approach. Mrs Doe had let it be known that her financial position was precarious. Due to an oversight, or in deliberate revenge for several years of domestic unhappiness, her husband had failed to arrange access for her to the not inconsiderable assets which were held in his name in foreign banks. Mrs Doe had written to the American President, appealing for help; after all, her husband had been a good friend and ally of the United States. She had difficulty in meeting her children's school fees, and her only property was her London house. Surely, this was not an appropriate fate for the wife of a man who, not long before, had been fêted at the White House?

To Mrs Doe, coming from a country where it was possible for everyone to know everyone else, and where the personal was hardly to be distinguished from the political, the American President's failure to reply must have seemed an act or omission of rank ingratitude, if not worse. No doubt it enabled her to think of herself as a victim, a condition to which almost all of humanity now aspires; but it did not improve her financial situation.

I therefore wrote offering a fee, but to this letter also I received no reply. On reflection, I think Mrs Doe was as correct in her judgement to ignore my letter as the American President had been to ignore hers.

Another Liberian exile in England, an interview with whom might have provided a suitable ending to my book, was Charles Taylor's brother-in-law who, I was informed, was playing the saxophone in a London musical. Unfortunately, my informant was not able to tell me which musical; and when I came to look at the list of London theatres, I discovered to my horror that the majority of them were staging musicals (a genre which is to drama what Taylor's movement is to freedom). Devoted as I am to writing, I was not prepared to attend thirty musicals to find which of them included a Liberian saxophonist in its orchestra.

A third possibility presented itself when a small newspaper item caught my eye (and imagination). Samuel Doe's private aircraft, a Boeing 707, was being exhibited to potential buyers at Stansted Airport in Essex. Its price was $9,000,000. What better poetic symbol for the Liberian civil war could there be than the aircraft, with its pink interior, a perfect union of limitless funds and appalling taste, of expense and frivolity? I called the airport to ask permission to see it, and was referred to the vendor's agent.

I made no pretence of being a man on the lookout for my very own Boeing 707: I admitted I was writing a book about Liberia, and was curious to see inside the ex-presidential craft. The agent saw no reason why I should not be allowed to do so, but said he would first have to ask permission – a formality – of someone he called 'the aircraft's principal' in Switzerland.

Permissions which are mere formalities are rarely granted; and several phone calls to the agent produced only the assurance that, once permission came from Switzerland, the agent would contact me. I knew, of course, that no such contact would ever be made; and so the interior of the Boeing – the metaphorical, if not the literal, possession of which was the only discernible purpose of the civil war – was destined to remain fixed in my imagination, forever pink velours, satin and leatherette.

I need not have despaired of finding a suitable conclusion, however. I had a letter from West Africa which informed me that Serge had been reconciled with the President of Togo, having suspected that Prince Johnson harboured 'unfriendly plans for him'. Rambo had been sacked by Monty Jones for shooting at the mice in Monty's bar in Lomé, the King's Head, with his revolver. Rambo frightened the customers away and did considerable damage to the bar, but the mice escaped unharmed. And a well-wisher in Monrovia, apprised of my enthusiasm for the work of C. Plato Warner, sent me – not through the post, since there was none – his latest mimeographed work entitled 'From Human Skulls to Freedom'. It is only fitting, then, to conclude with the words of Liberia's praise-singer of democracy:

> When politicians cry out for social change in Liberia
> Everybody jumps up and cries, 'We want change!'
> Yes, Liberia must have a democratic change;
> Liberia must have an efficient economic change;
> Liberia must have political change.
> Liberia needs all the fine changes
> That all free societies need to glorify democracy.